FLOYD CLYMER'S MOTORCYCLIST'S LIBRARY

The Book of the NORTON

A FULLY ILLUSTRATED PRACTICAL HANDBOOK FOR OWNERS AND PROSPECTIVE BUYERS OF NORTON MOTOR-CYCLES

(COVERS MODELS FROM 1932 ONWARDS)

BY

W. C. HAYCRAFT

F.R.S.A.

ANNOUNCEMENT

By special arrangement with the original publishers of this book, Sir Isaac Pitman & Son, Ltd., of London, England, we have secured the exclusive publishing rights for this book, as well as all others in THE MOTORCYCLIST'S LIBRARY.

Included in THE MOTORCYCLIST'S LIBRARY are complete instruction manuals covering the care and operation of respective motorcycles and engines; valuable data on speed tuning, and thrilling accounts of motorcycle race events. See listing of available titles elsewhere in this edition.

We consider it a privilege to be able to offer so many fine titles to our customers.

FLOYD CLYMER
Publisher of Books Pertaining to Automobiles and Motorcycles

2125 W. PICO ST.   LOS ANGELES 6, CALIF.

INTRODUCTION

Welcome to the world of digital publishing ~ the book you now hold in your hand, while unchanged from the original edition, was printed using the latest state of the art digital technology. The advent of print-on-demand has forever changed the publishing process, never has information been so accessible and it is our hope that this book serves your informational needs for years to come. If this is your first exposure to digital publishing, we hope that you are pleased with the results. Many more titles of interest to the classic automobile and motorcycle enthusiast, collector and restorer are available via our website at www.VelocePress.com. We hope that you find this title as interesting as we do.

NOTE FROM THE PUBLISHER

The information presented is true and complete to the best of our knowledge. All recommendations are made without any guarantees on the part of the author or the publisher, who also disclaim all liability incurred with the use of this information.

TRADEMARKS

We recognize that some words, model names and designations, for example, mentioned herein are the property of the trademark holder. We use them for identification purposes only. This is not an official publication.

INFORMATION ON THE USE OF THIS PUBLICATION

This manual is an invaluable resource for the classic motorcycle enthusiast and a "must have" for owners interested in performing their own maintenance. However, in today's information age we are constantly subject to changes in common practice, new technology, availability of improved materials and increased awareness of chemical toxicity. As such, it is advised that the user consult with an experienced professional prior to undertaking any procedure described herein. While every care has been taken to ensure correctness of information, it is obviously not possible to guarantee complete freedom from errors or omissions or to accept liability arising from such errors or omissions. Therefore, any individual that uses the information contained within, or elects to perform or participate in do-it-yourself repairs or modifications acknowledges that there is a risk factor involved and that the publisher or its associates cannot be held responsible for personal injury or property damage resulting from the use of the information or the outcome of such procedures.

WARNING!

One final word of advice, this publication is intended to be used as a reference guide, and when in doubt the reader should consult with a qualified technician.

PREFACE

THE author has aimed at providing a standard work of reference for Norton owners and prospective buyers, and has spared no pains to make it as complete as possible. He has in preparing this book derived a pleasure second only to that which actual Norton riding experience on a Model 18 has given him. What Norton ownership means is not fully grasped until it is realized. Especially is this so if one has hitherto been accustomed to the handling of smaller and less powerful motor-cycles.

Norton machines are very high grade and, without exception, very fast and powerful. In consequence, they are perhaps mainly the choice of the man who has served his apprenticeship on smaller machines and, desiring to pursue the healthy sport of motor-cycling, wishes to purchase a really sound and reliable mount with a high-power reserve and exceptional structural strength. In this handbook, therefore, the experienced rider is borne well in mind, and he will find all information he is likely to need on the subjects of lubrication, ignition, carburation, engine adjustments, electric lighting, and general overhauling matters. Pre-1947 O.H.C. engines are fully dealt with. In connection with the racing type engines, the reader will find much useful information and some notes in the last chapter on " Tuning for Speed," which it is hoped may be of some value and is, anyway, worth perusing.

For the benefit of the absolute novice (and the Norton is quite suitable for him owing to its flexibility and low revolution tickover) the author has included in Chapter II a few driving hints. The legal aspect of driving has not been touched on, mainly because laws are now constantly being altered.

Special attention is directed to Chapter IV dealing with " Lubrication." It should always be remembered that lubricating oil is the " life-blood " of an engine and, this being so, with a valuable and fine machine like the Norton, nothing should be left to chance in this respect. With the present efficient lubrication systems employed, the attention required from the rider is small indeed, which is all the more reason why that attention should be exact and never neglected.

Full instructions are given in this manual for the maintenance and running of the Lucas electrical equipment, and this should enable those readers who have no knowledge of electrical apparatus to understand and tend their lighting sets.

PREFACE

The fifth edition of *The Book of the Norton* contains *all essential information on driving and maintenance for owners of* 1932-47 *Nortons inclusive.* It does *not* deal, however, with the 1947 O.H.C. "International" spring-frame Models 30, 40, or with the racing "Manx" and Trials machines used for special purposes.

In a later edition of this handbook it is hoped to cover fully the 1947-8 "Internationals" (very similar to pre-1947 models dealt with), also the completely redesigned engines being fitted on the 1948 S.V. and O.H.V. Nortons. These machines (see page 19) are, except for their *new S. V. and O. H. V. engines*, almost identical to the corresponding 1947 types illustrated and fully dealt with in the present edition.

More petrol in the future and trouble-free running are the author's wishes for readers of this book. For those who may require replacement parts, some useful information is given on page 134.

Finally, it is only fair that the author should mention that he has no present or past connection with Norton Motors, Ltd., to whom he is much indebted for valuable assistance in the compilation of this manual. He is also indebted to Messrs. Joseph Lucas, Ltd., in regard to illustrations.

W. C. HAYCRAFT.

CHISWICK, W.4.

CONTENTS

CHAP.		PAGE
I. THE NORTON MODELS	. . . . .	1
II. DRIVING	. . . .	20
III. THE AMAL CARBURETTOR	. . . .	30
IV. LUBRICATION	. . . . . .	40
V. LUCAS ELECTRIC-LIGHTING EQUIPMENT	.	50
VI. ADJUSTMENTS AND OVERHAULING .	. .	60
APPENDIX .	. . . .	100
INDEX	. . . .	136

The Book of the
NORTON

CHAPTER I
THE NORTON MODELS

THE Norton has for many years been predominant in the motorcycle world. Every buyer of a machine designed and manufactured by Norton Motors, Ltd., of Bracebridge Street, Birmingham, 6, knows, and is proud of the fact, that he possesses a mount having marked simplicity combined with superb finish, first-class reliability, tremendous speed, and above all real stamina. The last-mentioned has been acquired thanks largely to the foresight of the makers in entering their machines in high speed road races throughout the world.

Perfection Through Racing. An immense amount of valuable data has been obtained in the arena of road racing and has been analysed and design revised accordingly. Standard models sold to the public incorporate the fruits of Norton racing successes. Who can forget the unique series of victories? Those who followed the T.T. races before the Second Great War will remember the Unapproachable Norton capturing the *first six places* in the Senior and Junior Manx Grand Prix races. Finally, in 1938 H. L. Daniell roared over the Island course at an average speed of 89·11 m.p.h., Nortons thereby winning the Senior T.T. for the seventh time in eight successive years! When war broke out the Norton went into action in the cause of justice. In June, 1947, Norton riders came home 1st, 2nd, 4th, 5th, 6th, 7th in the Senior T.T., and 1st in the Senior Clubman's T.T.

The Norton at War. War tests to the limit both metal and mettle! Nortons and their riders came through the test with colours flying. Approximately 100,000 Nortons (mostly high ground clearance 16H models) were produced to the Ministry of Supply requirements. These were distributed throughout the Fighting Services, and served under the most gruelling conditions. As on the Isle of Man, they mostly finished the course, even when bereft of many minor fittings. Among their duties were: dispatch carrying, patrol work, convoy escort, traffic control.

The Post-war Models. The author strongly advocates a visit to the nearest Norton agent, so that a close inspection can be made of the magnificent post-war models, which have a gleaming black and chromium finish. Their sturdiness and powerful

(*Auto Press Pictures*)
Fig. 1. Predominant In and Through Racing
A Norton rider in challenging mood, which recalls stirring memories of terrific duels in "The Island."

appearance strike the eye immediately. The 1946 range comprised two well-tried favourites, the famous S.V. Model 16H and the O.H.V. Model 18. The 1947-8 range includes also: a S.V. "Big Four," Model 1; the O.H.V. Model ES2 (with spring frame); two O.H.C. "International" Models 30, 40; two "Manx" racing versions of Models 30, 40; and two Trials O.H.V. Models 350T, 500T. All 1948 S.V. and O.H.V. engines are redesigned.

MODEL 16H (1939-47 SPECIFICATION)

This popular side-valve Norton has the following specification which applies in part to the whole 1939-47 Norton range—
The 4·90 h.p. S.V. Engine. Simplicity and robustness of construction are the keynote of this engine, whose design is similar to the "Big Four" power unit and has many features common

THE NORTON MODELS

to all Norton engines. It is an orthodox, vertical, four-stroke, single-cylinder unit, with a bore and stroke of 79 mm. and 100 mm. respectively, giving a cubic capacity of 490 c.c. and an A.C.U. rating of 4·90 h.p.

The principal features in its design are the provision of a detachable cylinder head with the valves below the level of the head and with the adjustable tappets and valve springs enclosed

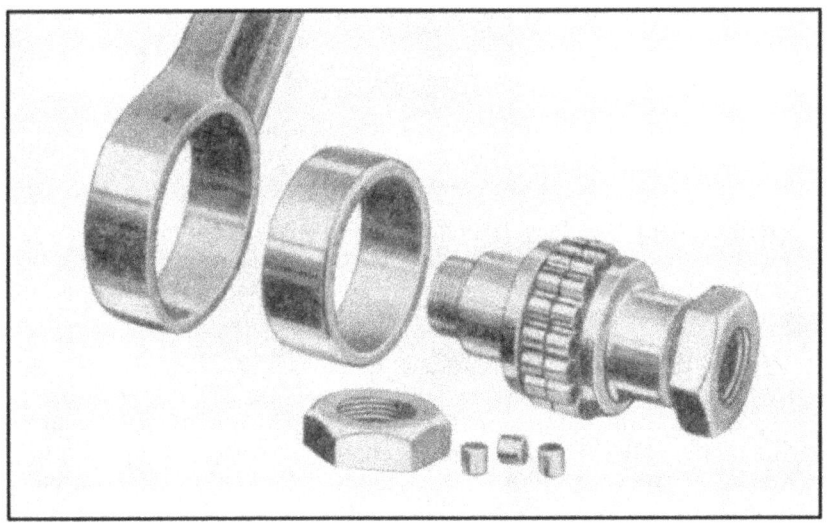

Fig. 2. The Sturdy Big-end Bearing

in a cast valve chamber; a twin camwheel timing gear with a much improved tooth form on the gears reducing load to the absolute minimum; a crankshaft assembly comprising flywheels with one roller and one ball bearing for the driving side mainshaft and a single roller bearing for the timing side mainshaft, a shouldered crankpin; an "H" section connecting rod with double-row roller big-end and fully floating hollow $\frac{7}{8}$ in. diameter gudgeon-pin in the small-end, an aluminium alloy piston giving a compression ratio of 4·9 to 1 and provided with three rings (the lower a scraper ring); a single exhaust pipe leading to a silencer of new design; a mainshaft engine breather.

Lubrication (All Models Except CSI, CJ, 30, 40). Full dry sump (see page 17) with twin gear pump forcing oil under pressure to the bearings and piston, which has no adjustable feed. An oil filter is incorporated in the pipe union to remove impurities. but no oil indicator is included on the timing case. Practically no attention need be given to the engine lubrication system. Automatic lubrication is provided for valve guides and overhead rockers.

Carburettor (**All Models Except 30, 40**). Amal semi-automatic needle-jet instrument with twist-grip control and throttle stop.

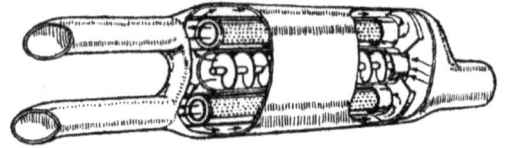

(*From "The Motor Cycle"*)
Fig. 3. The 1938 Spiral Baffle Silencer

Ignition and Lighting (**All Models**). Current is generated by a Lucas "Magdyno" with compensated voltage control. The instrument is placed behind the cylinder and chain driven off the half-time shaft. An electric horn is standard.

Frame and Forks (**All Models Except ES2, CSI, CJ, 30, 40**). Both are of Norton design and manufacture, the 1939 frame being of the semi-loop, and the forks a girder type with central spring and with hand-adjusted shock absorbers and rebound springs. A steering damper is included. The 1946-47 16H has a cradle frame of immense strength, built of high grade steel tube. All 1947 models have telescopic type front forks.

Handlebars (**All Models**). These are heavily chromium-plated and are insulated from road shocks (1939 models) by a rubber mounting (Fig. 4). Outside type levers are provided for the clutch, front brake and exhaust valve-lifter.

Gearbox and Clutch (**All Models**). The gearbox is of Norton design and is pivot mounted. Positive type foot control is fitted. On the 1946-47 models an outer cover conceals the whole of the clutch and positive foot change mechanism. The gears which are of large proportions provide the following ratios on Model 16H—

Solo . . 1st, 14·5 to 1; 2nd, 8·65 to 1; 3rd, 5·92 to 1; 4th, 4·9 to 1.
Sidecar . 1st, 16·2 to 1; 2nd, 9·65 to 1; 3rd, 6·6 to 1; 4th, 5·45 to 1.

The clutch, which has six friction plates and three springs, runs totally enclosed and has Ferodo inserts and hand adjustment. A vane type of shock absorber with rubber blocks (see Fig. 54) is incorporated in the clutch body.

Transmission (**All Models**). The primary chain, which measures $\frac{1}{2}$ in. × ·305 in., runs enclosed in a hermetically sealed oil-bath, while the secondary chain, which measures ⅝ in. × ·25 in., has a large protective guard and is lubricated by oil mist from a breather. Renold and Coventry chains are used exclusively, and the only shock-absorber provided is that incorporated in the clutch.

Brakes (All Models). Internal expanding Ferodo lined brakes of 7 in. diameter and 1¼ in. wide are fitted to front and rear wheels. Both brakes have finger adjustment.

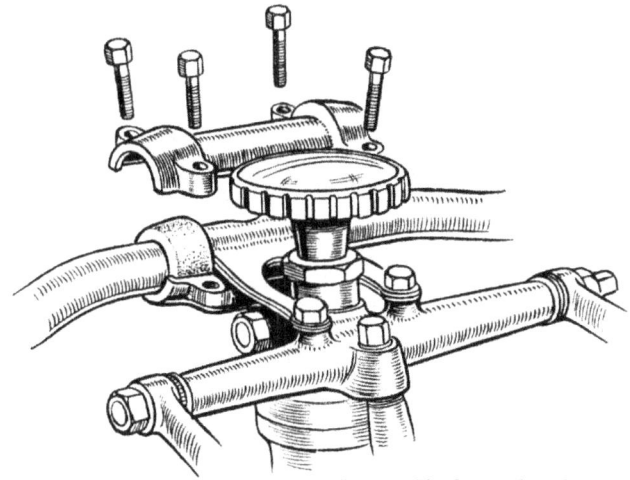

(*From "The Motor Cycle"*)
Fig. 4. The Insulated Handlebars (1935-9)

Wheels and Tyres (All Except 30, 40). Both wheels are of sturdy build with finest quality steel rims and heavy gauge spokes. The rims are chromium-plated with black centres lined out in red. Journal type bearings are used, that on the brake side being of the double-row rigid type. A new pattern hub is used with exposed wheel fixing bolt (Fig. 38). Both wheels, which are quickly detachable and interchangeable, are shod with 26 in. × 3.25 in. (3.25-19) Dunlop "Universal" tyres.

Mudguards (All Except 30, 40). Dust and road filth are effectively kept down by car type, pointed section mudguards of generous proportions. Mud channels are incorporated and the rear mudguard tail-piece is detachable to facilitate tyre removal.

Petrol Tank (All Except 30, 40). The tank is of the saddle type and made of welded steel. It has a capacity of 2¾ gal. and quick replenishment is assured by a new type of filler cap which is hinged to prevent its being lost. Finish is in lacquered chromium with handsome enamelled side panels. New rubber insulation is fitted and on 1939 models provision is made for a flush-fitting instrument panel which houses the ammeter, lighting switch, and speedometer. 1946-47 models have no provision for an instrument panel. The Smith speedometer (extra) is fitted on top of the front forks in a small panel set well forward.

Oil Tank (All Models). This is also of welded steel and 4 pints capacity to ensure the constant circulation of a large volume of oil throughout the engine. Finish is in chromium with suitable lining and a sump is incorporated in the base to collect foreign matter which can be drained away by removing a plug situated at the lowest point in the sump. The usual quick-release filler cap and gauze filter are included.

Saddle (All Models Except 30, 40). The saddle is a flexible top type with the springs attached to the chain stays and has forward pivotal mounting. It not only provides extreme comfort but also gives a very low riding position which enhances the naturally good road-holding qualities of the machine and inspires confidence in the rider.

Stands (All Models). Stands of the usual type are provided for both wheels, and in addition a new design of low-lift prop stand is fixed to the rear chain stays. This readily-operated stand greatly facilitates parking the machine and requires little physical effort to bring into use.

Footrests (All Norton Models). Comfortable rubber footrests with adjustable supports are provided, and lugs for pillion footrests are incorporated on the frame.

Tool Box (All Models). A very roomy all-metal tool box is neatly housed between the rear chain stays on the off side, and contains a comprehensive tool kit, a 15 in. × ⅞ in. tyre inflator, a grease gun, and a canister of grease.

MODEL I (1939-47)

The specification of this powerful sidecar machine differs from the 16H specification to a small extent as follows—

The 6·33 h.p. Side-valve Engine. The bore and stroke, instead of measuring 79 mm. × 100 mm., are increased to 82 mm. × 120 mm. respectively, giving a capacity of 633 c.c. and an A.C.U. rating of 6·33 h.p. Owing to the bigger stroke, and the fact that a reasonably low compression ratio is desirable for a general purpose machine specially built for sidecar work, a flat and not a domed head piston is employed. The compression ratio on the "Big Four" engine is 4·5 to 1.

THE NORTON MODELS

Gear Ratios. The gear ratios provided on the four-speed gearbox are the same as for Model 16H. Both the gearbox and clutch are of the same design and foot control is specified as standard.

An improvement to the foot control on recent Nortons is the neutral indicator and pedal designed to give easy gear changing without having to remove the foot from the rest.

MODEL 18 (1939-47)

The specification of Model 18, which is the only 1946 Norton overhead-valve model, differs from the 16H specification given on page 2 as follows—

The 4·90 h.p. Overhead-valve Engine. This has the same straightforward design as the standard 16H engine and has precisely the same bore and stroke, namely, 79 mm. × 100 mm., giving a cubic capacity of 490 c.c. and an A.C.U. rating of 4·90 h.p. The brake horse-power on full throttle is, of course, enormously in excess of this figure. Many of the parts are interchangeable with other O.H.V. engines.

The crankcase and timing case are similar in design to the S.V. type, and the flywheel assembly is similar. Roller bearings with shouldered crankpin are used for the big-end of the connecting rod and a plain bearing for the small-end, which takes a $\frac{7}{8}$ in. diameter fully floating gudgeon pin. The three-ring domed top piston provides a compression ratio of 6·6 to 1. The detachable cylinder head which fits direct on to the barrel has a combustion chamber of roughly semi-spherical shape with a single exhaust port discharging into a chromium-plated pipe and new design silencer. The driving side has a ball and roller bearing.

The lubrication arrangement, and also the magneto drive and valve-timing gear, show no appreciable differentiation from the 16H engine. Even the inlet and exhaust cams are of the same type and have the same valve timing. It should be noted that on the 1939 Model 18 and some O.H.C. engines, extra speed for racing can be obtained by fitting a special high compression piston supplied by Norton Motors, Ltd.

Details of the valve gear and rocker-box are clearly shown on page 60, where the compact new type of rocker-box is shown with the covers removed. The hollow-headed tulip pattern valves which are of nickel-chrome steel and have hardened bases to their stems, reciprocate in long hardened guides pressed into the cylinder head. Duplex coil valve springs are used, and they are anchored to the valve stems by split collets and conical-shaped collars. The lower halves of the valve springs are housed in two

Fig. 5. Model 16H (1946)

Fig. 6. Model 18 (1947)

Fig. 7. Models I 16H. (1947)

wells formed in the cylinder head casting. Two other castings which seat on the top of the cylinder head constitute distance pieces between the rocker-box and head. The rocker-box is a one-piece aluminium casting except for the end covers giving access to the new type of adjustment at the top of the push-rods which are enclosed in tubes socketed into the rocker-box with rubber oil sealing joints. The rockers have long bearings which are positively lubricated. Rocker-box lubrication is quite automatic and the feed controlled very precisely. Valve guides, O.H. rockers and valve stem ends are lubricated through internal ducts, no exterior pipes being used since 1937. Flat base cam followers are employed, the steel push-rods resting direct in cupped recesses. This considerably reduces mechanical noise. All timing gears have wide teeth.

Gear Ratios. The gearbox and clutch are exactly the same as on Model 16H, but the ratios are different. They are—
Solo . . 1st, 13·8 to 1; 2nd, 8·2 to 1; 3rd, 5·61 to 1; 4th, 4·64 to 1.
Sidecar . 1st, 15·3 to 1; 2nd, 9·12 to 1; 3rd, 6·24 to 1; 4th, 5·15 to 1.

Frame. On the 1939 Model 18 the frame is of the semi-loop pattern as used on the side-valve machine of the same year, but the 1947 version on Model 18 has a cradle frame similar to that provided on the 1946 O.H.V. model. It is extremely strong and very similar to that used on pre-1946 ES2 machines.

MODEL 19 (1939)

The specification of the most powerful push-rod operated O.H.V. Norton is identical to that of Model 18, except for a few points given herewith.

The 5·96 h.p. Overhead-valve Engine. The stroke of this engine is 13 mm. greater than that of the 4·90 h.p. O.H.V. engine, while the bore is 3 mm. greater. With a bore and stroke of 82 mm. × 113 mm., the cubic capacity is 596 c.c. and the rated horse-power 5·96. A piston with a 5·75 to 1 compression ratio is fitted as standard but may be changed for one of the high-compression type if preferred, although with its big capacity it is an engine capable of undertaking any gruelling work, solo or sidecar.

Gear Ratios. These are the same as for Model 18.

MODEL 20 (1939)

This machine has a specification identical to that of Model 18, except for the following small differences—

Two-port Engine. The bore and stroke are the same as on the single-port engine, namely, 79 mm. and 100 mm., and the capacity is, of course, 490 c.c. The compression ratio (6½ to 1) is also unchanged. The only difference between the two power units is that whereas Model 18 has a single-port cylinder head, Model 20 has a two-port type of cylinder head, well finned and designed to give rapid and smooth exit of the exhaust gases. The twin exhaust pipes terminate in spiral baffle silencers. As might be expected, the machine is wonderfully silent and a trifle faster than the single-port model.

MODELS 50, 55 (1939)

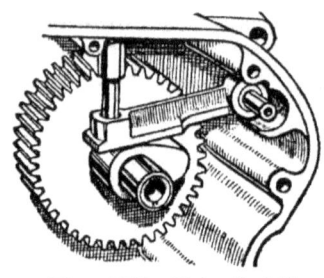

(*From "The Motor Cycle"*)
FIG. 8. 1938-47 FLAT BASE CAM FOLLOWER (S.V., O.H.V.)

These two machines have made a strong appeal to adherents of the 350 c.c. class, who desire a really lively type of machine with plenty of stamina. Models 50, 55 are identical, except that Model 55 has a two-port cylinder head. The general specification on page 2 applies to both machines, the differences being as follows—

The 3·48 h.p. O.H.V. Engine. This is a push-rod operated power-unit with a bore and stroke of 71 mm. × 88 mm., and a compression ratio of 7 to 1. Its design is similar to the 4·90 h.p. engine and includes dry-sump lubrication (no adjustment) and automatic rocker feed, a mainshaft engine breather, improved shape ports (inlet offset), a rear "Magdyno," a three-ring grooved aluminium alloy piston with ⅞ in. diameter fully floating gudgeon-pin secured by wire circlips, lubricated valve guides, cams of better profile with improved tooth form. The two-port cylinder head is similar to that used on Model 20 and the overhead rocker-box and valve gear are similar to those described for Model 18. The tulip pattern valves which have duplex springs are operated by steel push-rods resting in sockets on the toggle levers.

Gear Ratios. The four-speed Norton gearbox, which is fitted with foot control as standard, gives the following solo ratios—

1st, 15·35 to 1; 2nd, 9·14 to 1; 3rd, 6·25 to 1; 4th, 5·16 to 1.

Petrol Tank. Of welded steel with the usual finish, this has a capacity of 2¾ gal.

MODEL ES2 (1939-47)

The remaining push-rod O.H.V. model has a specification similar to that of Model 18, but a spring frame is standard.

THE NORTON MODELS

Fig. 9. Model 50 (1938)

Fig. 10. Spring Frame Model ES2 (1947)

Fig. 11. Models C.S.1, C.J. (1938)

Frame. This is an immensely strong structure of the triangulated cradle type, and is an improved version of the cradle frame originally adopted for use on the T.T. racing machines. Like all Norton frames, it is built of the finest quality high tensile steel, has graduated section lugs, and is constructed in jigs throughout to avoid any possibility of misalinement during manufacture. Rear-springing details shown in Appendix.

MODEL CSI (1939)

This fast and trim looking "camshaft" had a general specification as described on page 2, the major differences being in regard to the power-unit, frame, and gear ratios.

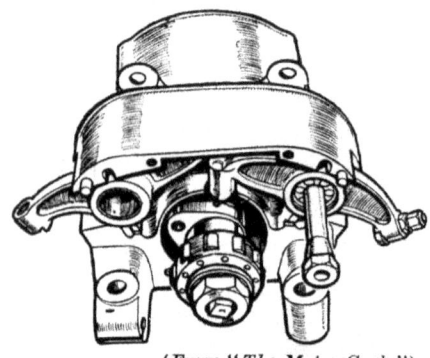

(*From "The Motor Cycle"*)

FIG. 12. SHOWING OVERHEAD CAMSHAFT AND ROCKERS

The 4·90 h.p. Overhead-camshaft Engine. The bore and stroke are 79 mm × 100 mm., giving a capacity of 490 c.c., and the compression ratio is 7 to 1. The flywheel assembly as on all other Norton engines is carried on three bearings (a ball, roller bearing on the driving side and a roller bearing on the timing side) and is housed in an aluminium alloy crankcase ribbed for stiffness. The big-end of the connecting rod differs from the O.H.V. engines in that a special type of caged roller bearing is used. The small-end has a $\frac{7}{8}$ in. diameter fully floating gudgeon-pin, and the piston is of the domed head type with a grooved skirt and three rings (the lower a scraper ring). The tulip valves are contained in a single-port cylinder head and are automatically lubricated from the rocker-box which, like the crankcase, is of aluminium alloy. The camshaft (Fig. 12) has two caged roller bearings and operates the valves through one-piece rockers with needle roller bearings and line contact adjuster pads, and is driven from the engine mainshaft by means of a vertical shaft and two pairs of bevel gears. Oldham couplings are used for the vertical shaft and vernier adjustment is provided for the camshaft bevel gear.

Lubrication (CSI, CJ, 30, 40). Full dry sump as on the S.V. models and O.H.V. models, but with certain differences (see page 40). A rotary gear pump with three sets of gears is driven from the engine half-time shaft and forces oil under pressure to the

THE NORTON MODELS

bearings and piston, the feed to the latter being adjustable. An auxiliary feed is also taken to the rocker-box for camshaft, rocker, and valve guide lubrication. Pump functioning can be verified by an oil indicator. In the base of the crankcase is an additional sump to remove impurities and the oil tank has a gauze filter.

Ignition (CSI, CJ, 30, 40). A Lucas "Magdyno" was usually supplied but for racing purposes a Lucas racing magneto or a B.T.-H. magneto can be fitted.

Frame (CSI, CJ, 30, 40). This is a triangulated cradle structure of immense strength similar to that used on Model ES2. It is built in jigs throughout and the cradle is raised at the nose.

Gear Ratios. The four-speed Norton gearbox, which has pivotal mounting, positive stop T.T. type foot control and a multi-plate clutch with vane type shock-absorber, provides the following gear ratios—
Solo . . 1st, 13·76 to 1; 2nd, 8·2 to 1; 3rd, 5·61 to 1; 4th, 4·64 to 1.
Sidecar . 1st, 15·35 to 1; 2nd, 9·14 to 1; 3rd, 6·25 to 1; 4th, 5·16 to 1.

Petrol Tank (CSI, CJ). The chromium-plated, welded steel saddle tank, which is provided with knee grips and an improved form of filler cap, has a capacity of $2\frac{3}{4}$ gal. A flush-fitting instrument panel could be specified if desired.

MODEL CJ (1939)

This machine is practically identical to Model CSI, except for reduced engine capacity and different gear ratios.

The 3·48 h.p. Overhead-camshaft Engine. This exhibits no radical departure from the 4·90 h.p. O.H.C. engine either in design or construction, but the bore and stroke are 71 mm. and 88 mm. respectively, giving a capacity of 348 cc., and the compression ratio is 7·4 to 1.

Gear Ratios. The four-speed Norton gearbox, which has foot control, provides the following solo gear ratios—
1st, 15·35 to 1; 2nd, 9·14 to 1; 3rd, 6·25 to 1; 4th, 5·16 to 1.

MODELS 30, 40 (1939 " INTERNATIONAL ")

The difference between Models 30, 40, and the other two O.H.C. Models CSI, CJ, is that the former incorporate many special features suited for serious racing, i.e. continual running at

Fig. 13. Trials Machine (1947 350,500 c.c.)

Fig. 14. Spring Frame "International" Models 30, 40 (1947)

Fig. 15. Spring Frame "Manx" Models 30, 40 (1947)

80 m.p.h. and over. All "International" engines are specially tuned and a special racing specification, including a light alloy cylinder head, was obtainable as an extra. Below is given briefly the standard "International" specification for 1939.

The 4·90 h.p. and 3·48 h.p. "International" O.H.C. Engines.

The 490 c.c. and 348 c.c. specially tuned engines have a bore and stroke of 79 mm. × 100 mm. and 71 mm. × 88 mm., and the compression ratios are 7·5 to 1 and 7·8 to 1 respectively. The general design of the "International" engines is similar to the CSI type and includes the improvements made to that engine (see page 12). It has a similar ribbed crankcase of nickel-aluminium alloy containing a flywheel assembly with caged double-row big-end bearings, a three-ring grooved aluminium alloy piston with hollow, tapered section ⅞ in. diameter, fully floating gudgeon-pin, dry sump lubrication with adjustable feed to the piston and oil tell-tale on the crankcase side, Oldham couplings for the vertical shaft, a camshaft running in caged roller and ball bearings with nickel-chrome steel rockers having sleeve adjusters with pads giving line contact on the valve stems. There are, however, many important differences.

An improved design of cylinder-head with torque stays, based on the latest racing practice, is fitted. This head has the finning and port shape determined with the greatest precision to give cool running and high thermal efficiency. Special attention has been paid to the finning near the exhaust port, which is inclined to the off-side. To expedite at high r.p.m. charging of the hemispherical combustion chamber (which will take a 14 mm. plug) a down-draught racing T.T. carburettor is flange-fixed direct to the inclined and offset inlet port. Both ports are streamlined and highly polished, and the very high grade steel valves used are lubricated automatically by a feed from the rocker-box. For road use the exhaust gases are discharged into a standard Norton silencer (single pipe), but if a straight-through pipe as supplied for racing is fitted, higher engine r.p.m. are possible, and the maximum speed is increased considerably. Actually the cylinder-head, valve timing, and cam contours are arranged for running with a straight-through exhaust. High-compression pistons, giving a C.R. of 10·5 to 1, 11·5 to 1, may be fitted for running on alcohol fuels, in which case 100 m.p.h. or over may be obtained. On 1939 "International" engines hairpin valve springs (see page 63) are fitted.

Carburettor. The flange-fitted down-draught caburettor is a special road racing T.T. semi-automatic Amal with twist-grip throttle control and external lever-controlled air slide. Fuel is fed to the float chamber by two Petroflex pipes converging to a

"T"-piece. For ordinary road work the recommended carburettor setting is for Model 30, a size 310 main jet used in conjunction with a 107 needle jet and middle needle position. In the case of Model 40, a size 260 main jet and a 107 needle in the same position are advised. When racing with a straight-through exhaust, different settings are required (see page 39).

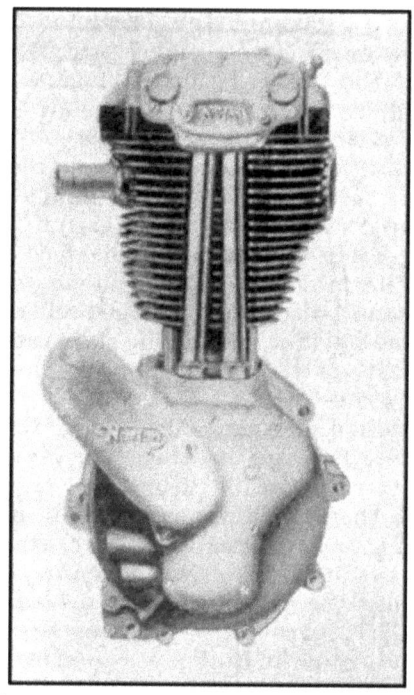

FIG. 16. AN ENGINE WITH A PEDIGREE—THE 1938–47 O.H.V. PUSH-ROD POWER UNIT

Cleanliness of design and "potted power" are the chief characteristics. 1938–9 improvements included redesigned rocker-box (Fig. 34); push-rod adjustment for the valve clearances; flat base cam followers (Fig. 8); wider timing gear teeth; a crankcase with all sharp corners removed. The lubrication system has been slightly modified. Similar improvements have been made to the S.V. engines, which have valve chests insulated from the cylinder by air passages. 1948 engines are redesigned.

Ignition. For touring purposes a Lucas MS1 "Magdyno" (without instrument panel) may be fitted, and for racing a B.T.-H. magneto is fitted as standard. The magneto or "Magdyno" is chain-driven anti-clockwise by sprockets off the rotary pump shaft.

Frame and Forks. These are similar to those used on the ES2 and CSI models, except that the triangulated short wheel-base frame has a ground clearance of only 3¾ in. The forks are of standard pattern with rebound springs and hand-adjusted shock-absorbers. A spring frame was available.

Gearbox, Clutch, and Transmission. The gearbox is a four-speed Norton box similar to that fitted on the other models, except that it is a special T.T. type with large diameter shafts and gears made of nickel-chrome alloy steel. Positive stop, quick operating foot control is provided, and unless otherwise specified, a kick-starter is fitted. With a kick-starter the gear ratios on Model 30 are: 10·8, 6·16, 5·1, 4·64 to 1. Without a kick-starter the bottom gear ratio is 7·86 to 1. On Model 40 without a kick-starter the gear ratios are 12·4, 6·87, 5·67, 5·16 to 1. With a kick-starter, bottom gear ratio is 12·4 to 1. The clutch is a three-spring six-plate shock-absorber type with Ferodo inserts, similar to the other clutches. The transmission is also the same as on the other models and includes an oil bath chain case or racing guard as specified.

Tanks. The special T.T. fuel tank, which is chromium-plated and suitably lined, holds 3¾ gal. (3½ gal. Model 40). Large sports type knee-grips are fitted to the sides, and two taps are provided, feeding the carburettor through a "T"-piece. An extra large chromium-plated T.T. oil tank holds 3 quarts. Both tanks have quick-release filler caps and Petroflex pipes.

Brakes, Wheels, and Tyres. Internal expanding Ferodo lined brakes, measuring 7 in. × 1¼ in., similar to those on other models, are provided, and there is finger adjustment on the off-side of the forks. The wheels differ from those on the other Nortons in that a type of front hub is used with the front brake drum and hub shell integral, and they are fitted with 27 in. × 3 in. ribbed front and 27 in. × 3·25 in. triple-studded rear Dunlop "Universal" tyres.

1938–47 LUBRICATION SYSTEMS

Two different type dry sump lubrication systems are used on Nortons. Details are shown in Figs. 17 and 17A.

On S.V. and O.H.V. Engines. The dry sump system is similar to that employed up to the end of 1937 and described on page 42, but a few important modifications have been made. It is now designed to supply automatically the correct amount of oil under all conditions to all parts. The twin gear-type pump (Fig. 26) draws oil from the tank and forces it through the restriction jet in the timing cover and the drilled mainshaft to the big-end bearing. Oil exuding from this bearing splash lubricates the piston and cylinder. An auxiliary oil feed is taken to the rear

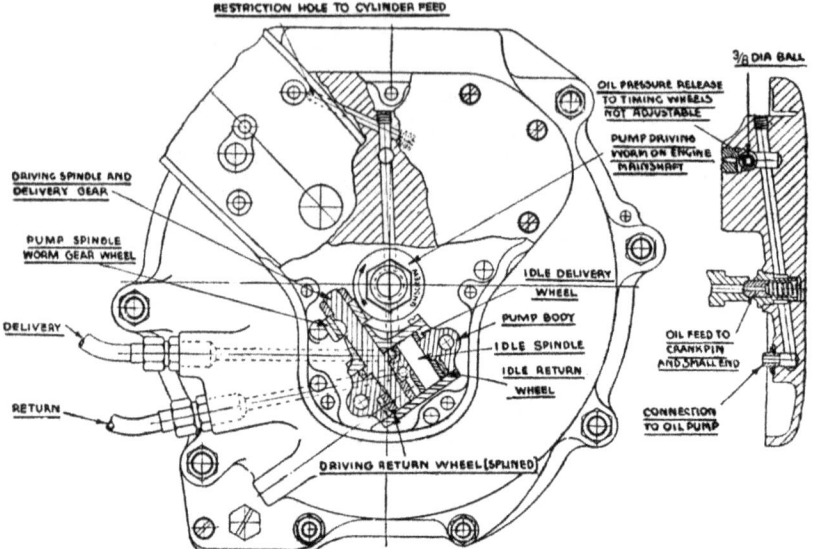

Fig. 17. 1938–47 Dry Sump System (S.V. and O.H.V. Engines)

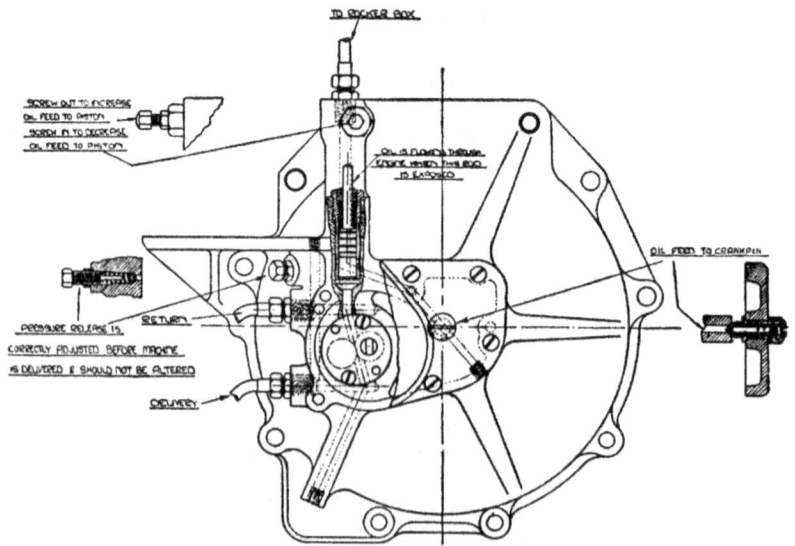

Fig. 17A. 1938–39 Dry Sump System (O.H.C. Engines)

THE NORTON MODELS

of the cylinder and also to the cam gear. The cylinder feed, however, no longer has a regulating screw and the oil indicator (Fig. 27) has been omitted. Oil after circulation through the engine collects at the bottom of the crankcase, which has a sludge trap, and is drawn by the return side of the pump and forced back into the oil tank. The tank has a gauze filter incorporated in the pipe union (Fig. 28) and a drain plug at the base.

On S.V. engines grease nipples for the valve guides (Fig. 27) are no longer provided, the valves being completely enclosed in a valve chest and lubricated by a jet with two small orifices protruding from the crankcase. In the case of the O.H.V. engines there are also no grease nipples provided for the rocker-box as hitherto, the rockers, valve ends, and valve guides being lubricated automatically, as mentioned on page 9, by oil mist.

On O.H.C. Engines. On all overhead camshaft models the dry sump system incorporates a rotary pump with three sets of gears. Its design is the same as that used previously and fully described on page 40. An exterior pipe feeds the rocker-box and the cylinder feed adjustment and oil indicator have been retained.

THE 1948 NORTONS

All the attractive 1947 Norton models are being continued for 1948. The four O.H.C. "International" and "Manx" Models 30, 40 (with spring frame) are completely unchanged. The general specification of the two S.V. Models 16H, 1, and the two O.H.V. Models 18, ES2 is also unaltered, except for the provision of an 8 in. diameter domed glass for the headlamp, which improves appearance and illumination. In appearance the 1948 S.V. and O.H.V. models are almost indistinguishable from the corresponding 1947 types illustrated in this chapter; but appearance is deceptive.

New S.V. and O.H.V. Engines. Norton Motors, Ltd., do not often redesign their engines from top to bottom, but the 1948 S.V. and O.H.V. models incorporate engines which have been redesigned so thoroughly as to make them for all practical purposes *new* engines. The new engines have modified crankcases, thicker flywheels of smaller diameter, a redesigned twin-camwheel timing gear, flat-base tappets, shorter push-rods, longer-skirt pistons, new one-piece rocker-boxes, and redesigned cylinders and cylinder heads.

The bore and stroke of each of the new engines remain as hitherto, but the result of the redesigning is a further improvement in power output, smooth running, and mechanical silence.

CHAPTER II

DRIVING

IN writing this chapter the author realizes that the majority of Norton riders are fully experienced and need little instruction on driving matters. Nevertheless there is a small minority who are

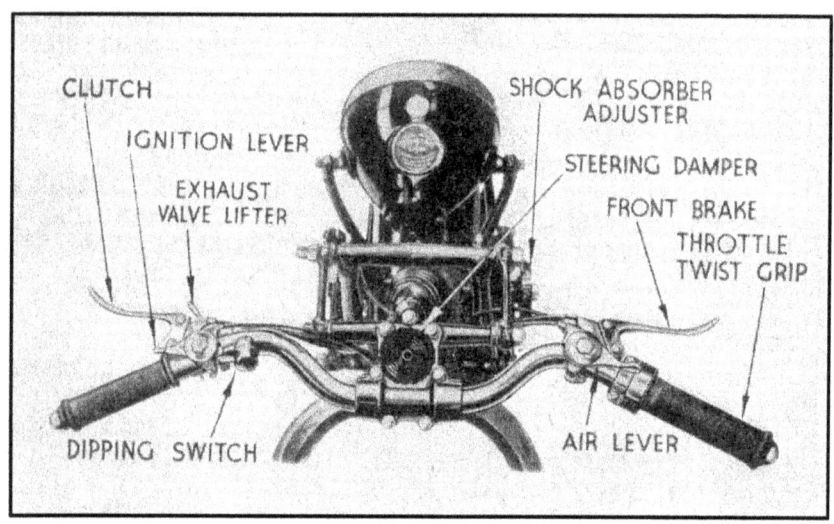

FIG. 18. SHOWING THE CONTROL LAY-OUT (1935 ONWARDS)

about to ride Nortons and, perhaps, to take to the road for the first time. It is for their benefit mainly that the following notes are compiled. These notes are somewhat limited in scope, but the author makes no pretence of dealing comprehensively with the subject of driving, nor does he deal with the various preliminaries which have to be attended to prior to putting a new machine on the road. It is presumed that the reader is familiar with these matters. If he is not, there is some other suitable literature available.

The Norton Controls. A view of the handlebar controls on all the Nortons is shown in Fig. 18. The arrangement is very neat, and the use of clip fittings enables the position of the controls to be varied if it is found that any of them do not come readily to

DRIVING

hand. There are four engine controls, namely, the throttle twist-grip, the air lever, the ignition lever, and the exhaust valve lifter. The throttle and air lever are opened by inward movement. The ignition is also advanced by inward movement (i.e. towards the rider). Exhaust valve lifter is now at the rear of bars.

Fuel and Oil Replenishment. Petrol benzole mixture is strongly recommended for all Norton engines, although petrol alone is satisfactory. Anti-detonating fuels are not necessary, and their advantages are of doubtful importance. Fifty-fifty petrol-benzole mixture is a suitable racing fuel for the "International" models, but it should be noted that the so-called fifty-fifty mixture obtainable from pumps can seldom be compared to a genuine fifty-fifty mixture. For racing, a rider is advised to mix it himself or to obtain it in sealed cans. If it is desired to run an O.H.V. or O.H.C. model on an alcohol fuel, a special high-compression piston may be needed. The Norton fuel tank has at its base a decent-sized gauze filter, but never neglect to use a funnel with a filter when replenishing from a can, as impurities are apt to form a sediment at the tank bottom and interfere with free supply to the engine, due to the tank filter becoming stopped up.

Always replenish the oil tank with the correct grade of oil and make recommended by Norton Motors, Ltd. (see Chapter IV), and refuse stolidly, if you value your engine, the "just as good" brand which some garages supply from bulk and recommend for everything from a traction engine to a two-stroke. Before checking the oil level, run the engine a few minutes to scavenge the sump. The oil level in the tank should not be above approximately 2 in. from the top of the filler cap (or the tank more than three-quarter full on post-war models), and should never be allowed to fall below the half-way level in the tank.

Always Maintain Correct Tyre Pressures. All Dunlop tyres are now fitted with Schrader valves and, with the aid of a pressure gauge, the pressure can be measured accurately. The author recommends the Dunlop Pencil Type No. 6 gauge, illustrated in Fig. 20. This gauge is extremely convenient as it has a clip to fit the waistcoat pocket. To use this gauge, the valve dust cap (Fig. 19) is taken off, and the end of the pressure gauge is pressed on to the open end of the valve. It depresses the pin and allows air to enter the gauge and push up the piston calibrated in pounds per square inch. It is always wise to keep the dust caps screwed on, though some riders throw them away! Dust or grit getting into the valve stem is liable to interfere with the valve action of the little spring-controlled plunger (Fig. 19) and cause leakage. About once a year valve "insides" should be replaced. They can be removed by taking off the valve cap and using the slotted end as a screwdriver.

The Norton has been aptly described as "The World's Best Road Holder," but this is true only if the tyres are kept correctly inflated. Correct solo pressures for 26 in. × 3·25 in. (3.25-19) tyres are 18 lb. per sq. in. for the front tyre and 23 lb. per sq. in. for the rear tyre, where telescopic front forks are fitted. On machines with girder type front forks, inflate front and rear tyres to 16 and 24 lb. per sq. in respectively.

To Start Up (1932 Onwards). Turn on the petrol and on 1932–4 models turn the circular milled oil tap to the "full on" position.

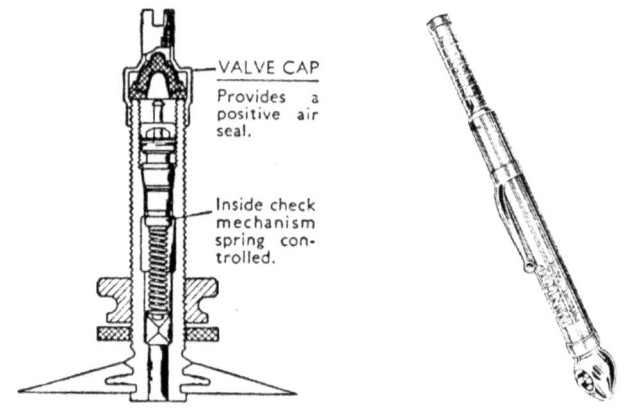

FIGS. 19, 20. SHOWING (LEFT) DUNLOP VALVE AND (RIGHT) POCKET PRESSURE GAUGE

Never omit to verify that this oil tap is turned on before starting up. When leaving the machine idle the tap need not be turned off but it is advisable to turn the tap off when the machine is left for any considerable period. Recent models have no tap.

Slightly flood the carburettor and proceed thus: Place gear lever in neutral; open the throttle from one-quarter to one-eighth of its total movement; close air lever completely or, if the engine be warm, open it about one-eighth; and retard the ignition lever until it is midway between full advance and full retard. The forementioned correct settings are dependent, of course, upon there being no backlash in the controls. The slightest perceptible movements of the twist grip and air lever should commence to lift the carburettor slides. Unless this is the case, sensitive engine control is impossible, and engine performance greatly handicapped. Difficult engine starting is usually attributable to faulty control

DRIVING

setting, and it cannot be too strongly impressed how important it is to *keep the throttle lever nearly closed* when endeavouring to effect a start. Only by so doing can a high velocity air stream be induced over the pilot jet of the Amal carburettor provided in 1932 onwards. This point can be realized by referring to Fig. 21.

If the engine is unduly stiff due to the congealing of oil, it will be advantageous to free the piston, to depress kick-starter crank without lifting the exhaust valve lifter until resistance of compression is felt, raise exhaust lifter and depress kick-start crank a further 1 or 2 in.; allow crank to return to its upright position and, without lifting exhaust valve lifter, depress kick-start crank as smartly as possible. This procedure allows sufficient petrol vapour to be sucked in to thin down the oil film slightly. But never prime an engine with neat petrol.

To start the engine, stand astride the machine, put the piston on compression, raise the exhaust valve lifter, depress the kick-starter with a vigorous kick, and drop the lifter when the crank is about three-quarters down. With the engine and carburettor in proper order, a start should be effected on the third kick at the most. Failure to start quickly is usually due to some definite defect, and generally ignition trouble; and the plug should be removed, inspected, and, if necessary, cleaned and the points adjusted. (See page 63.)

A prevalent source of engine-starting difficulties is an over-rich mixture caused by excessive intentional flooding of the carburettor or by numerous ineffectual attempts with the kick-starter, made worse perhaps by a low temperature. To clear the combustion chamber of vaporized fuel, open both throttle and air lever to their full extent and revolve the engine several times.

Once the engine has sprung into life, adjust the controls to give a sweet "pilot" tick-over. Advance the air lever fully, or nearly fully, and similarly advance the ignition lever. Resist the temtation to "rev" the engine up *until the oil is circulating properly and has warmed up*. Sudden engine racing, especially when not under load, is most injurious and entirely unnecessary, and subjects the engine to large stresses and unduly high temperatures, which cannot be dissipated. Never continue to run an engine in a closed garage, as carbon monoxide, a dangerous product of combustion, may "send you off" before you realize the danger. If a dry sump lubricated engine starts to issue clouds of blue smoke when starting up, ignore this phenomenon, as the surplus oil will quickly be returned to the tank by the pump. Under no circumstances reduce the supply by turning off a tap. If smoking continues, cut down the oil supply to the piston on 1932–7 models. Black smoke denotes an over-rich mixture. Instructions for tuning the carburettor will be found on page 33.

Check Oil Circulation After Starting Up. This can be done by removing the oil filler cap and observing whether froth is present on the surface of the oil due to the ejection of oil from the return pipe. Also take a look at the oil indicator on 1932-7 models, and note whether the plunger has risen. Failure of the plunger to rise shows that the oil pump is not functioning satisfactorily.

Moving Off. Raise the clutch (when both gear-box mainshaft and layshaft become idle), depress the foot change to engage first gear, and allow the transmission to take up the drive by progressively and gently letting-in the clutch, while slowly increasing the throttle opening. As soon as possible fully advance the ignition. Note that first gear is obtained when the indicator has moved fully *anti-clockwise*.

Change from First to Second Gear. The knack of gear-changing on a motor-cycle is rapidly mastered, and gear crashing of a serious nature is impossible owing to the special design of the Norton gear-box, where all pinions are of the constant mesh type. Speed up the machine until about 12 m.p.h. is attained, declutch, and simultaneously throttle the engine down, wait a second until mainshaft and layshaft are running at the same speed, and depress the foot change, afterwards letting in the clutch gently and throttling up again to take the increased load. *Never employ force on the foot change.* All operations should be quick, but accurate, and progressive, and *no attempt should ever be made to change gear without first declutching*, for in this case we have dog clutches being induced to mesh while being *driven* at different speeds. *On no account allow the engine to knock* (i.e. make a metallic noise) by driving it too slowly under load or with too advanced ignition timing. Knocking is both the cause and the effect of a worn engine, and, if allowed to continue, usually results in fracture of some part. A change to a lower gear should be made immediately the engine shows signs of distress, *but do not slip the clutch as an alternative to gear-changing.*

Change from Second to Third Gear. Proceed as before. Speed up the machine until it has plenty of momentum, declutch, throttle down, wait a second and smartly move the foot change home into third gear, afterwards throttling up again until the desired speed is reached.

Change from Third to Fourth Gear. To get into top gear, follow the previous procedure. Throttle up, declutch, ease off the throttle, wait momentarily and move the foot change into fourth gear. The tendency for knocking, if any, is during the change

DRIVING 25

from third to fourth, and the controls should be handled judiciously to counteract this, especially if the change is made on an up-gradient, when the engine revolutions should be kept high during the changes. When changing up on a down grade, or even on the level, if care be taken, the foot change may be moved right through the gears from first to fourth. Only experienced riders, however, should adopt this method.

Change from Fourth to First Gear. Throttle down until the machine is travelling at a speed at which it normally does on bottom gear, lift the clutch and raise the foot change into first gear position.

Be Careful with Foot Control. The foot-control lever has a very considerable leverage and, to avoid damage to the gear selectors and control mechanism, it must not be used roughly. When changing gear, depress or raise the lever *gently*, according to the gear required, by movement of the *toe* and do not lift the foot from the pedal *until the clutch has been re-engaged*. If you are taking over a new mount, remember that the lever always returns to the *same position* after every gear change.

Always Run on a Good Plug. The importance of this cannot be overstressed. On S.V., O.H.V., and O.H.C. models with 18 mm. plugs fit a Lodge H1 or H1P, or a K.L.G. M80. For racing on "International" type models with 18 mm. plugs, a Lodge R18 is recommended. Lodge H14S or K.L.G. F70 plugs are strongly recommended, for all 1937 and later models with 14 mm. plugs (i.e. all except the S.V. engines). On O.H.C. models, however, use a 14 mm. Lodge HNP (or HHN) or K.L.G. F70 (for racing fit a 14 mm. Lodge RL47 or RL51).

Removing Dynamo for Speed Work. When using an electrically-equipped O.H.V. or O.H.C. model for speed work, quite an appreciable gain in speed can be achieved by eliminating the power absorbed by the dynamo. The dynamo portion of the Lucas "Magdyno" fitted to Norton models can be detached by removing the strap holding it to the ignition portion of the generator.

Hand Signals. One of the most common causes of accidents is the failure of one or all parties concerned to give the proper hand signals, or to give them at the proper time. Last-minute hand-wagging is futile and most dangerous. All signals which are intended to convey anything should be clear, and should be given at a time when the following traffic is in a position to heed the warning without the screech of friction linings on brake drums.

Controlling Speed. The proper and usual method of controlling speed is by means of the throttle supplemented by an occasional touch, not jab, of the rear brake pedal. Continuous and violent application of the internal expanding brakes may provide thrills and enable a rider to scrape out of difficulties occasioned by bad judgment or recklessness, but it will gradually take the best out of the machine, and pile up bills for tyre and transmission renewals, even if it does not incur a bad debt for a telegraph post. The most experienced and best riders use their brakes to an extraordinarily small extent. They *drive on the throttle.*

A still more pernicious and to be pitied rider is the one who uses his exhaust valve lifter for checking speed round corners, with the difference that, instead of ill-treating his tyres and transmission, he burns and distorts his exhaust valve, a vital part of the engine.

Keeping an Engine Cool. Although all Norton engines are designed for speed and power, it is possible with any engine to cause overheating when driving on the low gears for long periods or when climbing very steep hills without allowing the engine a respite every now and then. Overheating is serious, as it may cause permanent damage to the valve seats or valves, or the seizure of a piston. To avoid overheating other than that caused by pre-ignition or faulty carburation, it is advisable always to (*a*) run with the spark well advanced; (*b*) see that lubrication is right; (*c*) give the engine as much air as it will take; (*d*) shut off the gas when descending hills after climbing.

Running-in. After taking delivery of a brand new Norton, certain care must be exercised for a period when driving. *Until* 500 *miles have been covered, a speed in excess of* 35 *m.p.h. in top gear should not be attained*; also see that the supply of oil (if it is adjustable) to the piston is on the liberal side. With regard to the question of running-in, it is important, besides avoiding excessive speed, to avoid opening the throttle more than one-quarter to one-third, and never to allow the engine to labour. The importance of the foregoing advice cannot be overstated, for if too liberal use of the throttle be made during the early life of the machine it will never attain that degree of efficiency that it should do, and its performance will be probably spoiled (see also page 49).

Running-in is vital for three reasons: (*a*) only by gentle friction can the crystalline metal surfaces become hardened and of uniform consistency; (*b*) until there are good running fits throughout the engine, it is impossible for oil to find its way in sufficient quantity over the bearing surfaces; (*c*) insufficient clearances will result in there being abnormal friction with the consequent risk of overheating, accompanied by distortion or burning occurring. It may be very tempting to try the "bus" out after 300 miles have been covered, but ask yourself the question, "Is it worth while?"

Piston Seizure. Ball and roller bearings are used for the crankshaft, and therefore piston seizure is the only kind of seizure likely to arise through over-driving a new machine which has not been thoroughly run-in. If piston seizure (indicated by sudden loss of power and gradual slowing up) should occur, whip out the clutch and throttle down instantly. Allow the engine to cool before continuing, and at the first opportunity examine the cylinder for score marks, which must be removed. Pre-ignition, due to an unsuitable plug, produces symptoms similar to those of piston seizure.

Cultivating "Feel." There is a huge difference between *driving* a machine and *riding* a machine, although a sidecar outfit cannot be ridden in the real sense of the word. *Driving* entails merely controlling and steering a machine, while *riding* implies exercising those faculties of balance, sight, and intuition which enable a man to become temporarily "a part of" the machine himself, as does a good horseman become "part of" his horse. To a man who rides his machine well, motor-cycling is as natural as walking, and far less strenuous! Quick reflex action is the most important quality, having regard to the question of the "feel" of a machine, although practice enables this to be cultivated.

Hill-climbing. The Norton is capable of surmounting any hills in England and most abroad. It is purely a question of making a fast climb, if this is desired. Hill-climbing requires power, and power is only possible with high engine revolutions. *The golden rule, therefore, in hill-climbing is to keep the "revs" high* without actually racing the engine. Engine racing, unless the clutch is slipping, is not likely to occur when hill-climbing, except in first gear; and the chief concern of the rider is, when driving on the other two gears, to keep the "revs" sufficiently high to enable the power output to be big enough to climb the gradient without changing down. A gear change should, however, be made immediately there is a serious and unavoidable decline in engine revolutions, and a change should be made while the machine still has plenty of momentum. Never carry on in top if this entails letting the "revs" fall away below 1,800 r.p.m., which corresponds to a road speed of about 30 m.p.h. in top gear. *The gear-box is designed for use and should be used.*

When hill-climbing, the carburettor controls should be used carefully. Gradually open the throttle as the gradient increases, and very gradually retard the ignition lever and change down immediately slight metallic noise warns the rider that the engine is commencing to labour. Retarding the ignition still further reduces power, so that this action should be delayed until quite necessary. Remember that down-coming traffic is always expected to give way to traffic going up, in the event of obstruction being caused. This is a matter of ordinary courtesy.

Descending Hills. There are several methods of doing this, viz. (*a*) coasting down with the clutch out or gear lever in neutral and the engine off or just ticking-over; (*b*) descending in gear with the throttle closed, or almost closed.

When descending in gear with the throttle practically closed and the air lever wide open, the engine compression acts as an exceedingly powerful brake, and this braking effect is still greater when the engine revolutions are increased by engaging a lower gear. It is advisable not to close the throttle entirely owing to the risk of causing a vacuum in the cylinder, which would result in oil being drawn past the rings and fouling the combustion chamber, with consequent plug trouble. After coasting in neutral with engine off (a very pleasant sensation), be careful not to re-engage a gear against full compression. The exhaust valve lifter should be used momentarily and the clutch let in gradually.

A Few Don'ts. The author would conclude this short chapter with a few "don'ts." In these days of ultra-rapid and constantly changing motoring legislation it is quite a problem to keep fully acquainted with what you must and must not do, and the safest course is to scan one of the motor-cycling weeklies or that part of your morning paper devoted to the cause of motoring. The following few don'ts have occurred to the author as being worth mentioning and are applicable at the moment of writing.

1. Don't forget your driving licence and insurance certificate.
2. Don't carry a pillion passenger unless he or she can be trusted to keep cool in emergency.
3. Don't omit to read the Highway Code.
4. Don't run with smooth tyres (this is an offence).
5. Don't make a noise in the lower gears.
6. Don't sound your horn between the hours of 11.30 p.m. and 7 a.m. (this is an offence).
7. Don't speed near "Belisha" crossings (pedestrians have right of way).
8. Don't forget when you are in a "built-up" area (30 m.p.h. limit).
9. Don't race traffic lights (i.e. don't cut across when amber follows green).

DRIVING

10. Don't go over "white lines."
11. Don't cut-in.
12. Don't drive on the brakes.
13. Don't flog your engine continuously.
14. Don't cross tramlines in front of lorries.
15. Don't fail to test brakes.
16. Don't fail to give hand signals *in time*.
17. Don't let your thoughts wander from driving.
18. Don't forget a speedometer is compulsory.
19. Don't refuse an S.O.S.
20. Don't forget you are only young once, and only live once.
21. Don't run with the near-side petrol tap on, or you will draw on the reserve supply.

MEMORANDA

Your Telephone No. ....

Norton Telephone No. .... *Aston Cross* 0776–0778............

Nearest Norton Agent ....

Insurance Co.'s Address ....

Insurance Policy No. ....

Your Registration No. ....

Engine No. ....

Frame No. ....

Date of Purchase of Machine ....

Mileage Done ....

New Tyres Fitted ....

Piston Rings Fitted ....

Rebushing Done ....

New Chains Fitted ....

Complete Overhauls ....

Decarbonizing ....

....

CHAPTER III

THE AMAL CARBURETTOR

GOOD engine performance naturally depends to a great extent on correct carburation. All Norton models are sent out from the works with the carburettors carefully tuned and with jet sizes giving the best all-round performance. In the ordinary way it is not wise to alter the maker's setting, but sometimes it is necessary to retune the carburettor, when, for instance, the original setting has been interfered with or the rider wishes to indulge in racing. In this chapter the author has given full information and tuning instructions for the two types of Amal carburettors fitted to the Norton range. These carburettors comprise the semi-automatic needle jet carburettor and the road racing carburettor.

The Two-lever Semi-automatic Carburettor (All Except " Internationals "). This carburettor has been practically unchanged for many years, and the advice given applies to all 1932 and later models. In order to tune the carburettor intelligently it is necessary to grasp how the instrument works.

How It Works. The carburettor fitted to all except the "International" engines is of the two-lever needle jet type, the mixture at slow or idling speeds being controlled by a readily adjustable pilot jet, whilst at higher speeds the mixture is controlled by means of a needle attached to the throttle slide and working in a restriction jet. The two-lever control must not be confused with the type of control that was used a considerable time ago on the two-lever carburettor, in which it was necessary constantly to adjust the air lever in accordance with the conditions under which the machine was running. This carburettor is for all practical purposes automatic, the air lever being closed only to facilitate starting and occasionally under very adverse circumstances. The carburettor slides are chromium plated to provide hard wearing surfaces.

Referring to Fig. 21, showing a sectional view of the instrument, A is the carburettor body or mixing chamber, the upper part of which has a throttle valve B, with taper needle C attached by the needle clip. The throttle valve regulates the quantity of mixture supplied to the engine. Passing through the throttle valve is the air valve D, independently operated, and serving the purpose of obstructing the main air passage for starting and mixture regulation. Fixed to the underside of the mixing chamber by the union nut E is the jet block F, and interposed between them is a fibre washer to ensure a petrol-tight joint. On the upper part

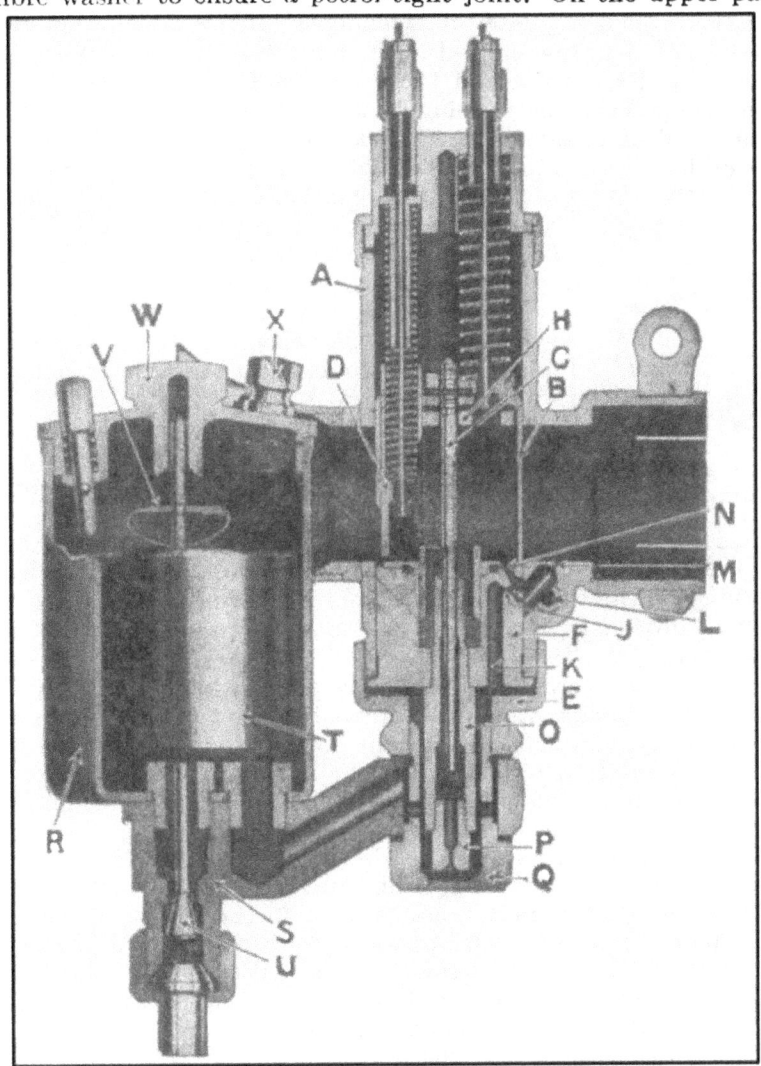

Fig. 21. Sectional View of Two-lever Needle Jet Amal Carburettor

of the jet block is the adaptor body H, forming a clean throughway. Integral with the jet block is the pilot jet J, supplied through the passage K. The adjustable pilot air intake L

communicates with a chamber, from which issues the pilot outlet
M and the by-pass N. An adjusting screw (TS, Fig. 21A) is provided
on the mixing chamber, by which the position of the throttle valve
for tick-over is regulated independently of the cable adjustment.
The needle jet O is screwed in the underside of the jet block, and
carries at its bottom end the main jet P. Both these jets are
removable when the jet plug Q, which bolts the mixing chamber
and the float chamber together, is removed. The float chamber,
which has bottom feed, consists of a cup R, suitably mounted on
a platform S, containing the float T and the
needle valve U attached by the clip V. The
float chamber cover W has a lock screw X for
security. (See also page 100.)

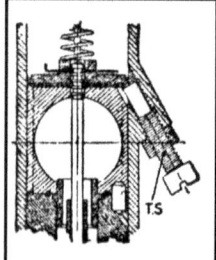

Fig. 21A. Amal Throttle Stop

The petrol tap having been turned on, petrol
will flow past the needle valve U until the
quantity of petrol in the chamber R is sufficient
to raise the float T, when the needle valve U
will prevent a further supply entering the float
chamber until some in the chamber has already
been used up by the engine. The float chamber
having filled to its correct level, the fuel passes
along the passages through the diagonal holes
in the jet plug Q, when it will be in communication with the
main jet P and the pilot feed hole K; the level in these jets
being, obviously, the same as that maintained in the float
chamber.

Imagine the throttle valve B very slightly open. As the piston
descends, a partial vacuum is created in the carburettor, causing
a rush of air through the pilot air hole L, and drawing fuel from
the pilot jet J. The mixture of air and fuel is admitted to the
engine through the pilot outlet M. The quantity of mixture
capable of being passed by the pilot outlet M is insufficient to
run the engine. This mixture also carries excess of fuel. Consequently, before a combustible mixture is admitted, throttle valve
B must be slightly raised, admitting a further supply of air from
the main air intake. The further the throttle valve is opened,
the less will be the depression on the outlet M, but, in turn, a
higher depression will be created on the by-pass N, and the pilot
mixture will flow from this passage as well as from the outlet M.
The mixture supplied by the pilot and by-pass system is supplemented at about one-eighth throttle by fuel from the main jet P,
the throttle valve cut-away determining the mixture strength
from here to one-quarter throttle. Proceeding up the throttle
range, mixture control by the needle position occurs from one-quarter to three-quarters throttle, and from this point the main
jet is the only regulation.

THE AMAL CARBURETTOR

The air valve *D*, which is cable-operated on the two-lever carburettor, has the effect of obstructing the main through-way and, in consequence, increasing the depression on the main jet, enriching the mixture.

Tuning the Amal Carburettor. Should the setting of this instrument not give entire satisfaction for particular requirements, there are four separate ways of rectifying matters as given herewith, and the adjustments should be made in this order: (*a*) Main jet ($\frac{3}{4}$ to full throttle). (*b*) Pilot air adjustment (closed to $\frac{1}{8}$ throttle). (*c*) Throttle valve cut-away on the air in-take

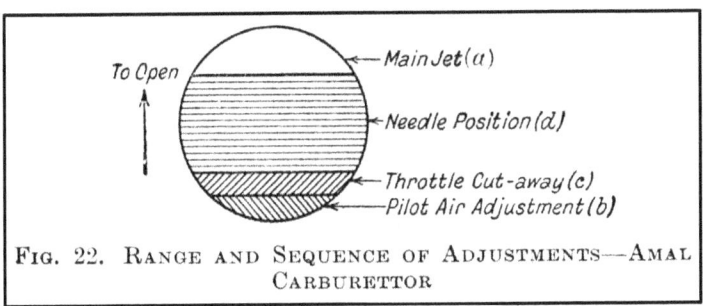

FIG. 22. RANGE AND SEQUENCE OF ADJUSTMENTS—AMAL CARBURETTOR

side ($\frac{1}{8}$ to $\frac{1}{4}$ throttle). (*d*) Needle position ($\frac{1}{4}$ to $\frac{3}{4}$ throttle). The diagram (Fig. 22) clearly indicates the part of the throttle range over which each adjustment is effective.

(*a*) To obtain the correct main jet size, several jets should be experimented with, and that selected should be the *smallest which gives maximum power and speed* on full throttle.

(*b*) To weaken slow-running mixture, screw pilot air adjuster outwards, and to enrich screw pilot air adjuster inwards.

Screw pilot air adjuster home in a clockwise direction. Place gear lever in "neutral." Slightly flood the float chamber by gently depressing the tickler until fuel begins to escape from the mixing chamber. Set ignition half advanced, throttle approximately $\frac{1}{8}$ open, close the air lever, start the engine, and warm up. After warming up, reduce the engine revolutions by gently throttling down. The slow-running mixture will prove over-rich unless air leaks exist. Very gradually unscrew the pilot jet adjuster. The engine speed will increase, and must again be reduced by gently closing the throttle until, by a combination of throttle positions and air adjustment, the desired "idling" is obtained. It is occasionally necessary to retard completely the ignition before getting a satisfactory tick-over, especially when early ignition timing is used. If it is desired to make the engine idle with the throttle quite closed, the position of the throttle valve must be set by means of the throttle stop screw, the throttle twist-grip during this adjustment being rotated to the fully-closed position. Alternatively, if the screw is adjusted clear of the throttle valve, the engine will be shut off in the normal way by the twist-grip. Do not take the throttle stop screw out completely.

(c) Given satisfactory "tick-over," set the ignition control at half-advance with the air lever fully open. Very slowly open the

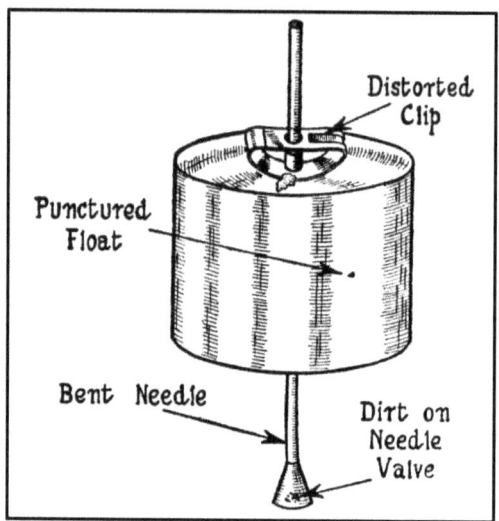

Fig. 23. Some Possible Causes of Persistent Flooding of the Float Chamber.

throttle valve, when, if the engine responds regularly up to one-quarter throttle, the valve cut-away is correct.

A weak mixture is indicated by " spitting back " through the air intake, with blue flames and hesitation in picking up, which disappears when the air lever is closed down. This can be remedied by fitting a throttle valve with less cut-away. A rich mixture is shown by a black sooty exhaust, and the engine falters when the air valve is closed. The remedy for this is a throttle valve with greater cut-away. Each Amal valve is stamped with two numbers, the first indicating the type number of the carburettor, and the second figure the amount of cut-away on the intake side of the valve in sixteenths of an inch, e.g. 6/4 is a type 6 valve with 4/16 in. or a ¼ in. cut-away.

(d) Open air lever fully and the throttle half-way. Note if the exhaust is crisp and the engine flexible. Close the air valve slightly below the throttle, when the exhaust note and engine revolutions should remain constant. Should popping back and spitting occur with blue flames from the intake, the mixture is weak, and the needle should be raised a notch. Test by lowering the air valve gently. The engine revolutions will rise when the air valve is lowered slightly below the throttle valve. If the engine speed does not increase progressively with raising of the throttle, and a smoky exhaust is apparent with heavy, laboured running, and tendency to eight-stroke, the mixture is too rich and the needle should be lowered in the throttle valve. Having found the correct needle position, the carburettor setting is now complete, and it will be found that the driving is practically automatic once the engine is warmed up. For speed work on petrol fuels the main jet may be increased by 10 per cent, when the air lever should be fully open on full throttle. If extreme economy is desired, lower the needle one groove farther after carrying out the four series of tests described above.

Possible Causes of Bad Slow-running. If it is found impossible to obtain good slow-running by making the pilot air adjustment as described in paragraph (*b*) on page 33, it is probable that some defect other than carburation is responsible for preventing the engine running slowly at low revolutions. Air leaks are a possible cause which should be looked for. They may be due to a poor joint at the carburettor attachment to the cylinder and/or a worn inlet valve guide. Badly seating valves will also weaken the mixture. Defects in the ignition system may also be responsible for poor tick-over. The sparking plug may be oily, or the points set too close (see page 63). Possibly the spark is excessively advanced or the contact-breaker needs attention (see page 64). Examine the slip ring for oil and see that the pick-up brush is bedding down and in good condition. Also examine the H.T. cable for signs of shorting.

For Racing. A genuine fifty-fifty petrol-benzole mixture is suitable used in conjunction with a high-compression piston, but for speed work an alcohol fuel such as R.D.I. gives perhaps the best results. Tune for speed and disregard fuel consumption. The main jet may be increased by about 10 per cent for speed work (much more for alcohol fuels). In the case of the overhead camshaft models it is best to substitute a special road-racing carburettor for the standard carburettor and tune it as described on page 37. This racing carburettor has been used by the Norton racing men with marvellous success in all the big international road races. It goes without saying that to obtain very high speeds, in addition to tuning the carburettor with great care, it is essential to tune the engine thoroughly, cut down weight where possible, and select the most suitable gear ratios for the particular purpose in mind. Some general hints on tuning for speed will be found on page 82.

Maintenance of the Amal Carburettor. Periodical cleaning is necessary to maintain efficient functioning of the carburettor, and should be carried out in the following sequence.

Disconnect petrol pipe. Unscrew holding bolt Q (Fig. 21) and remove float chamber complete. With box or set spanner, slacken the mixing chamber union nut E. Mixing chamber complete may now be removed from engine, simply by unscrewing the clip pin holding the carburettor on the induction pipe. Unscrew mixing chamber lock ring, and pull out throttle valve, needle and air valve. Remove main jet P and needle jet O. Mixing chamber union nut E may then be removed and jet block complete pushed out. If this is obstinate, tap gently, using a wooden stump inside the mixing chamber. Unscrew float chamber cover W and slacken lock screw X. Withdraw the float by pinching the clip V inwards, and at the same time pull gently upwards.

Generally it is sufficient to wash all the parts in clean petrol, but if the carburettor has had extended service, check the following—

(a) FLOAT CHAMBER NEEDLE U. If a distinct shoulder is visible on the point of seating, renew this as soon as convenient.

(b) THROTTLE VALVE. Test in mixing chamber, and if excessive play is present it is advisable to renew this without delay.

(c) THROTTLE NEEDLE CLIP. This part must securely grip needle. *Free rotation must not take place*, otherwise the needle groove will become worn and necessitate a new part being fitted. *Be sure to refit the clip in the same groove.*

(d) JET BLOCK. If trouble has been experienced with erratic "idling," ascertain by means of a fine bristle that the pilot jet J is clear, and that the pilot outlet M in the mixing chamber is unobstructed.

To Reassemble. Refit jet block F with washer on underside and screw on lightly mixing chamber union nut E. Screw in needle jet O and main jet P. Open air lever $\frac{7}{8}$ in., throttle lever half-way; grasp the air slide between the thumb and the finger; *make sure that the needle enters the central hole in the adaptor top.* Slightly twist the throttle valve until it enters the adaptor guide, when on pushing down the valves the air valve should enter its guide. If not, slightly move the mixing chamber top, when the air valve will slide into place. Screw on mixing chamber lock-nut. *No brute force is necessary.*

Attach carburettor to the cylinder, pushing right home, and examine washer if flange fitting. Insert holding bolt Q, and thoroughly tighten union nut E by means of a fixed spanner. Refit float and needle, holding the needle head against its seating by means of a pencil until the float and the clip V are slipped into position. Make sure that the clip enters the groove provided. Screw on the cover tightly and lock in position by means of the lock screw X. Fit holding bolt in float chamber with one washer above and one below the lug. Screw holding bolt into mixing chamber and lock securely. Clean petrol pipe and filter if fitted, and replace. It will be necessary to re-check the pilot setting if this has been disturbed.

THE NEEDLE JET ROAD-RACING CARBURETTOR (PRE-1947 " INTERNATIONAL " MODELS)

This carburettor (T.T. Model) is pre-war standard on the "International" Models 30, 40, but can also be fitted if desired on the overhead camshaft Models CSI and CJ. It has been designed with two main objects in view, high maximum speed and good acceleration. It is an ideal carburettor for all road-racing purposes.

Special Features. Exceptional care has been taken in the design and manufacture of the choke which is based on a long racing experience. The choke offers the minimum resistance to the passage of the ingoing mixture from the carburettor, and so enables the engine to develop the utmost power and acceleration of which it is capable. Good acceleration is further ensured by the provision of means for adjusting the mixture strength at all throttle openings and the incorporation of an adjustable pilot jet which enables the engine to respond instantly to a sudden turn of the twist-grip. A special feature of the racing carburettor is the use of an external air valve at the side of the mixing chamber. This affords ample means of regulating the mixture strength without creating any obstruction to the main gas pressure, and it is thus possible to compensate for variations in atmospheric conditions and altitude.

Tuning the Racing Carburettor. Tuning the T.T. racing carburettor involves procedure very similar to that employed for the standard two-lever semi-automatic instrument, and the tuning sequence is the same. Make the adjustments in this order: (*a*) main jet; (*b*) pilot jet adjustment; (*c*) throttle valve cut-away; (*d*) needle position.

(*a*) To determine the size of the main jet, experiment with several jets and select the smallest jet which gives the *greatest maximum speed*. The air lever should be fully open during these tests on full throttle.

(*b*) Before attempting to set the pilot adjuster the engine should be run to its normal running temperature, otherwise a faulty adjustment is possible which will upset the correct selection of the throttle valve. The pilot adjuster which controls the amount of petrol passed is rotated clockwise to weaken the mixture, and anti-clockwise to richen the same. The pilot adjuster should be adjusted very gradually until a satisfactory tick-over is obtained, but care should be taken that the achievement of too slow a tick-over (i.e. slower than is actually necessary) does not lead to a "spot" which may cause stalling when the throttle is very slightly open.

(c) Having set the pilot adjuster the throttle should then be opened up progressively and positions noted where, if at all, the exhaust note becomes irregular. When this is noticed the throttle should be left open at this position and the air lever slightly closed, which will then give an indication as to whether the "spot" is a rich or a weak one.

If it is a rich "spot," a throttle valve should be fitted with more cut-away on the air intake side, and *vice versa*.

(d) The needle position will affect carburation up to somewhere over one-quarter throttle, after which the jet needle, which is suspended from the throttle valve, comes into action, and when the throttle is opened further and tests are again made for rich or weak spots, as previously outlined, the needle can be raised to richen or lowered to weaken the mixture, whichever may be found necessary.

When the foregoing adjustments have been correctly made and the main jet size has been settled it will be found that a perfectly progressive mixture will be obtainable from tick-over to full throttle.

Size of Needle Jet. It is not necessary to alter the size of the needle jet when tuning, but before attempting to tune the carburettor the rider should make sure that the correct needle jet is fitted. In the case of Models 30 and 40 the correct size needle jet to use when running on petrol or petrol-benzole are ·109 and ·1075 respectively.

Alcohol Fuels. When alcohol fuel is used a needle jet size ·113 must be fitted, and it is also necessary to increase the main jet by the following amounts—

P.M.S.2 Fuel . 60 per cent greater flow than for petrol.
R.D.I. Fuel . 80 to 100 per cent greater flow than for petrol.

From the above it will be seen that it is necessary to convert the jet size to its flow in c.c.'s per minute according to the table on page 39, then increase the figure by the percentage recommended above and finally convert the number obtained back to the equivalent jet size number in the table. The jets on the T.T.

THE AMAL CARBURETTOR

TABLE OF JET DIAMETERS WITH EQUIVALENT FLOWS IN C.C.'s PER MINUTE

Jet Number	Flow in c.c.'s per Minute	Jet Number	Flow in c.c.'s per Minute
40	160	74	550
41	170	77	600
43	180	81	650
45	200	84	700
47	220	87	750
49	240	90	800
51	260	92	850
53	280	95	900
55	300	98	950
57	325	100	1000
59	350	105	1100
61	375	110	1200
63	400	115	1300
65	425	118	1400
67	450	122	1500
69	475	127	1600
71	500	130	1700

racing carburettor are marked in numbers indicating approximately the diameters, but the equivalent flow can be obtained from the table. For 1938-9 this flow is the jet number.

Use Larger Jets with Straight-through Exhaust. As already mentioned on page 16, the specially-tuned "International" Models 30, 40 are designed to give their maximum b.h.p. without a silencer fitted, and correct carburation under such conditions is of supreme importance. When racing a 490 c.c. "International" model on 50-50 petrol-benzole with straight-through 1¾ in. pipe fitted, a size 400 main jet with 109 needle jet is most suitable. In the case of a 348 c.c. "International," use a size 350 main jet and 107 needle jet. The needle should be in the middle position in both cases.

Jet Sizes for Alcohol Fuels (30, 40). When using alcohol fuel (e.g. R.D.I.) for "International" models, a size 700 main jet with a 113 needle jet will be found most suitable for the 490 c.c. engine, and a size 660 jet with a 113 needle jet for the 348 c.c. engine. In both cases the needle should be in the central position.

CHAPTER IV
LUBRICATION

THERE are many ways of ill-treating a motor-cycle, but none is so calculated to take effect quickly as failure to provide the right amount and kind of lubrication. Friction is both the enemy and the servant of the mechanical engineer. Without friction, brakes and clutches would be non-existent, and for that matter all motor vehicles would be non-existent, for they would be unable to travel along the road due to lack of grip. These are examples of the assets of friction. Now for the drawbacks. Friction throughout all the bearings and moving parts of both engine and machine incurs a definite loss of efficiency due to the transformation of energy into heat at the contacting surfaces, whereas the whole of it would be better employed in propelling the machine along the road. Further, under-lubrication results in the generation of sufficient heat to cause serious damage. A certain amount of friction is inevitable, but it can be very greatly reduced if riders will make full use of the lubrication system provided by the Norton designers. Lubrication, which consists of maintaining a microscopically thin film of oil at all contacting surfaces, can conveniently be divided into two groups: (*a*) engine lubrication; (*b*) cycle lubrication. Engine lubrication is far and away the most important and can never safely be neglected. We shall therefore consider this first.

ENGINE LUBRICATION

There are three main parts in the engine where lubrication is vital: (*a*) at that part of the cylinder bore traversed by the piston and the piston rings (which reciprocate at an average speed of about 30 m.p.h.); (*b*) the crankshaft assembly, including the two mainshaft bearings, and the big-end and small-end connecting-rod bearings; (*c*) the timing gear and the valve-operating gear. All these parts are automatically lubricated on all 1932 and later Norton engines by a full dry sump lubrication system. As has been mentioned on page 3, a gear type oil pump forces oil to the bearings and piston, and there are two types of pumps used, a twin type pump on the S.V. and O.H.V. engines and a triple type pump on the O.H.C. engines (including the "Internationals").

Dry Sump Lubrication (All O.H.C. Models). The lubrication system on the "camshafts" is a constant circulation type, which has been designed to give the correct amount of oil to all parts,

LUBRICATION

under all conditions, and little attention is necessary. Oil is drawn from an oil tank of large capacity which has a detachable filter incorporated in the feed pipe union and on 1932-4 models a tap which can be used if necessary to control the oil supply to the pump. It is not wise, however, to control the oil supply at this point, as an adjustable supply to the piston is provided. 1935

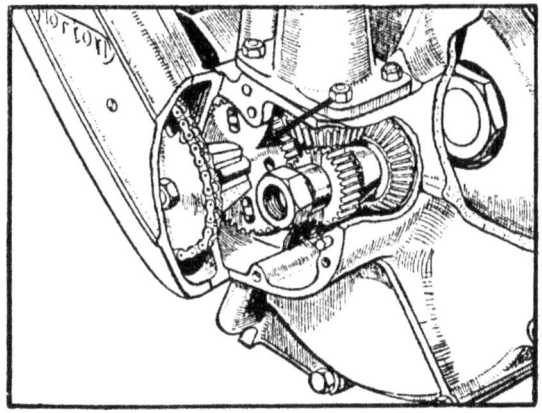

(From " The Motor Cycle")

Fig. 24. Spur Gear Drive for O.H.C. Oil Pump

and later models have a tank filter but no tap, the filter being incorporated in the feed pipe union (Fig. 28).

The oil pump, which is of Norton design and manufacture, is driven from a small spur wheel on the engine shaft, which meshes with a larger wheel in which slots are cut to engage with pegs on the pump driving member (Fig. 24), and may be withdrawn as a complete unit. (See page 95.) The pump is of the rotary gear type, with three sets of gears. It draws oil from the tank, and delivers it under pressure to the timing gear and big-end bearing via a restriction jet abutting the timing side hollow mainshaft, the hollow crankpin and flywheel, whence it is thrown by centrifugal force upon the cylinder and piston. Surplus oil drains to the sump, is purified, and returned to the tank.

Another lead is taken through passages and into a hollow bolt —one of those holding the two halves of the crankcase together. This bolt has small drillings which permit of oil passing through a small hole in the crankcase casting and thence into a groove running round the underside of the cylinder base flange. From this groove small drillings are made to the interior of the cylinder. The feed of oil to this point is adjustable by means of a hexagon-headed screw (Fig. 25), situated in the top rear corner of the crankcase. Just below this adjuster screw is an oil indicator tell-tale of the spring-loaded type similar to that on 1932-7 S.V. and O.H.V. engines (see Fig. 27). Its object is solely to show whether the pump is working and it does not *necessarily* indicate circulation. Oil is also fed under pressure to the rocker-box and camshaft, any surplus draining back through grooves in the

Fig. 25. Adjustable Feed to Cylinder
(O.H.C. Models)

vertical shaft, bevel gears to the base chamber. An external pipe is used to feed the rocker-box, and both valve guides are lubricated from the box.

Under no circumstances should the pump be dismantled, but if requiring attention (which is most unlikely) it should be returned to the makers for adjustment by an expert.

Dry Sump Lubrication (1932-7 S.V. and O.H.V.). On the S.V. and O.H.V. models a twin gear-type oil pump, which has two sets of gears and is constructed as a detachable unit (Fig. 26), is driven by means of a worm wheel on the pump driving spindle and a worm on the engine main shaft at $\frac{1}{14}$th engine speed, and after drawing oil from the tank forces it, as on the O.H.C. models, to the big-end and flywheels via a duct leading to a restriction jet fitted to the timing case cover and abutting the end of the drilled main shaft. Apart from splash lubrication, some of the oil is forced through ducts cast in the crankcase direct to the cylinder wall and piston skirt, with an adjustment provided in the form of a hexagon-head screw situated in front

LUBRICATION

of the magneto chain case on top of the timing case cover. Also situated on top of the timing case cover is a plunger tell-tale (Fig. 27) similar to that used on the O.H.C. engines. Some of the

FIG. 26. THE OIL PUMP (S.V. AND O.H.V.) WITH BOTH PAIRS OF GEARS REMOVED FROM BODY

oil flowing direct to the cylinder is by-passed to the timing gear, and in the case of the O.H.V. engines, oil mist from the timing case passes up the push-rod cover tubes and lubricates to some

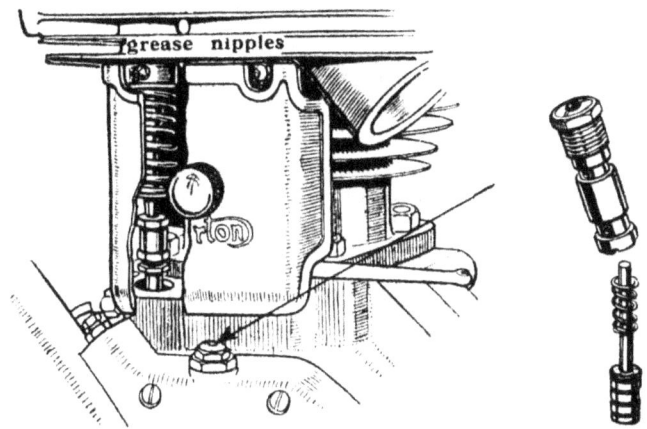

(*From " The Motor Cycle"*)

FIG. 27. SHOWING OIL TELL-TALE (1932-7 S.V. AND O.H.V.) AND VALVE GUIDE LUBRICATION (1936-7 S.V.)
Note the adjustable cylinder feed at the top left-hand corner of timing case.

extent the overhead rocker bearings. Grease-gun lubrication is, however, retained for these bearings. Two grease nipples are provided on the side of each rocker bearing boss and on the 1936-7 S.V. engines valve guide nipples (Fig. 27) are used. On 1934-7 O.H.V.'s the valves are automatically lubricated by oil mist passing along two small pipes leading from the rocker box. Surplus oil from the big-end and piston drains to the sump from which the large scavenge pump returns the oil to the tank. A sludge trap is incorporated in the base of the crankcase sump to trap particles of foreign matter. There is a filter on all 1932-7 models on the feed side of the pump in the tank itself. The tank filter is incorporated in the feed-pipe union and 1932-4 models have a control tap by which the oil feed to the pump can be controlled if necessary. 1935-7 models have no tap, but they have a filter and a drain plug at the base of the tank. For 1938-47 see page 17.

Suitable Engine Oils. As mentioned on page 21, the oil tank should be maintained at least *half-full*. During running-in it is beneficial to mix Colloidal Graphite with the engine oil (see page 49). If used subsequently, mix the compound in the proportions ½ pt. to 1 gallon. For touring purposes during the summer, on S.V. and O.H.V. models, use Patent Castrol "XXL," Mobiloil "D," Triple Shell, or Price's Motorine "B" de Luxe. During the winter use Patent Castrol "XL," Mobiloil "D," Double Shell, or Price's "C" de Luxe. With the O.H.C. models in summer and winter, use Castrol "R," Castrol "Grand Prix," or Price's "B" de Luxe.

Concerning Engine Lubrication. Very little attention indeed is required on 1932 and later dry sump models, and if the following instructions are carefully followed it is unlikely that any trouble will be experienced. See that the oil in the tank is kept at or above *half-full* level, and never run the engine with the tap, at the base of the oil tank (on 1932-4 models), turned to the "off" position. This tap may be left on when the machine is standing idle, but remember that with a pump that does not provide a good oil seal and in very hot weather the thinned oil may gradually pass the pump with the engine stationary.

To check the oil circulation, you must remove the tank-filler cap and notice whether there is froth on the oil surface caused by oil being ejected from the return pipe. On 1932-7 models it is possible to ascertain by a glance at the oil tell-tale (Fig. 27) whether the pump is functioning satisfactorily, in which case the small plunger is raised about $\frac{3}{8}$ in. It should be particularly noted, however, that the tell-tale provides no indication as to whether there is *sufficient* oil circulating, and the plunger may still rise even with the oil tank empty.

With regard to adjustment of the oil supply, if after 500 miles of careful running-in, a 1932-4 machine shows a tendency to over-oil, the oil tank control tap regulating the supply of oil to the pump may be adjusted accordingly. If a 1932-9 O.H.C. or a 1932-7 S.V. or O.H.V. engine is inclined to smoke continuously, the oil

LUBRICATION

fed direct to the piston skirt from the pump should be cut down by screwing in the adjustable hexagon head screw (situated at the top rear corner of the crankcase on O.H.C. models, and on the rear of the timing case on S.V. and O.H.V. models) until it is, say, one-half turn, or even one-quarter turn, from the "full-off"

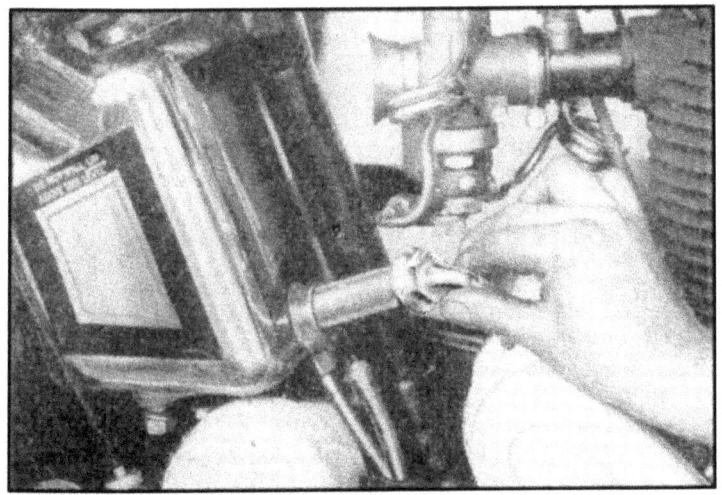

FIG. 28. REMOVING OIL TANK UNION AND FILTER

For 1935 onwards a drain plug is employed at the bottom of the oil tank, enabling the whole of the oil, including any sediment which may be at the bottom of the tank, to be readily drained off. This drain plug enables the oil tank to be drained without disconnecting feed pipe. Remove the filter as shown.

position (screwed right home). The correct adjustment for touring is usually one complete turn from the "full-off" position. Upper cylinder lubrication is unnecessary on any Norton engines, as hardened valve guides are used since 1932, and for 1932 onwards on O.H.V. models the guides are automatically lubricated, but lubricate the 1932-7 rocker-boxes. (See also page 101.)

Drain the Oil Tank Every 2000 Miles. On Norton engines with D.S. lubrication, the oil tank should be emptied and the tank and filter cleaned with petrol at least once every 2000 miles. In the case of a new engine, this should be done after the first 500 miles' running. On 1932-4 models the filter in the oil tank, attached to the feed-pipe union, must first be removed. To empty the tank and remove the filter, unscrew the large hexagonal union situated at the front of the tank, to which is attached the oil feed tap. This will allow the whole of the oil to be drained from the tank. When refixing the feed pipe, fit at the top end first, turn on oil, and do not attach the bottom union until the pipe is full. On 1935 and later models drain the tank by removing the base plug.

Drain Crankcase when Decarbonizing. It is advisable on all Norton models to drain and swill out the crankcase with flushing oil when decarbonizing; this is not essential. A rag should *always* be wrapped round the connecting rod so as to block up the hole when drawing off the barrel. (See page 74.)

Swill the engine out thoroughly. A good method is to refit the cylinder barrel temporarily and kick the engine over several times. The oil pipes must, of course, be disconnected, otherwise paraffin will be pumped into the tank. After swilling out, remove the sump plug and continue revolving the engine until all paraffin and oil are expelled. Before finally reassembling the cylinder, put some clean engine oil on the flywheels and on the sides of the piston.

Rocker-box Lubrication. Automatic rocker-box lubrication is to be found on 1932-9 "camshaft" and the 1938 and later O.H.V models, but a small amount of oil mist penetrates upward from the crankcase between the push-rods and their tubular covers on all 1932-7 O.H.V. models. Grease-gun lubrication for these rocker-boxes is provided, and attention should be given to them every 1000 miles when replenishing the gear-box with grease. The grease-gun included in the tool-kit should be used for injecting the grease at the nipples on the rocker-box bearing bosses.

Valve Guide Lubrication (1936-7 S.V.). On the 1936-7 S.V. engines the grease-gun should be applied every 800–1000 miles to the two nipples provided (Fig. 27). 1938 onwards—automatic.

Magneto and Magdyno Lubrication. The bearings of the machine are packed with grease before leaving the works, and no further attention is required until 15,000 miles are exceeded, when the bearings should be repacked by the manufacturer once more with grease. With the M-L magneto an occasional spot of oil should be applied to the cam surface. About every 5000 miles a few drops of thin machine oil should be put in the hole in the cam (which has a wick) or on the wick in the contact-breaker base in the case of Lucas ring cam and face cam type contact-breakers respectively. (See also pages 50, 86.)

THE CYCLE PARTS

Four-speed Gear-box Lubrication. Suitable lubricants for 1932–3 three-speed and 1933–47 four-speed gear-boxes are Wakefield's "Castrolease Medium," engine oil respectively. Grease is obtainable in collapsible tubes. When replenishing in the absence of a collapsible tube of grease, it is advisable, in order to inject it

LUBRICATION

through the lubricator, to liquefy the grease by warming it, and 50 per cent engine oil should be added to it. The correct level of lubricant in the four-speed gear-box is such that the layshaft is half submerged (i.e. the gear-box is about *one-third* full). An original charge of $\frac{1}{2}$ pint of engine oil is advised, and thereafter topping up about every 1000 miles should be sufficient. Do not forget to lubricate the clutch, gear control mechanism (including the foot-gear change) about once every 1000 miles. With regard to filling the gearbox, on no account use *thick* grease. Engine oil is the correct lubricant (see page 44) for all four-speed gearboxes. If you do not care about measuring fractions of a pint, recharge every 1000 miles with half a cupful of lubricant. This is near enough. Rotation with the kick-starter will assist replenishment. Grease occasionally the lever on the end of the foot pedal shaft. Drain and refill the gearbox every 5000 miles.

The Primary Chain. On 1932–3 models the primary chain is well protected and automatically lubricated with oil mist from a breather of the port type situated in the boss through which the engine main shaft protrudes. It is important to see that the breather functions properly and that the pipe leading from it is unobstructed. About every 3000 miles it is a good plan to remove the chain and clean it.

On 1934 and later Norton models the chain is contained in an oil bath chain case and is absolutely protected from dirt. The oil bath should be replenished about every 1000 miles with engine oil such as Castrol XXL. To replenish, remove the inspection cover from the top of the chain case and also the oil level plug from the bottom of the chain case. Then pour oil through the inspection cover hole until it reaches the level of the filler plug with the machine upright. Drain and refill ($\frac{1}{2}$ pint) every 1000 miles.

The Secondary Chain. Smear the chain with grease every 1000 miles. Engine oil can be used for the rear chain, and the best method of oiling is to rotate the chain with the wheel and apply an oil-gun or can to the top of the chain. See that the oil is falling upon the rollers, and not on the ground, and make a practice of oiling regularly. If the chain be neglected, undue wear of both chain and sprockets will ensue, and the transmission will be harsh. From time to time (say once every 3500 miles) take off the chain and give it a bath in paraffin. If allowed to soak well, the whole of the dirt will be extracted, and the chain may be hung up to dry and refitted. Before refitting, however, the wisest course is to immerse the chain in a receptacle containing a mixture of hot graphite grease and engine oil, which will then permeate all the roller bearings. There is no better treatment for a main driving

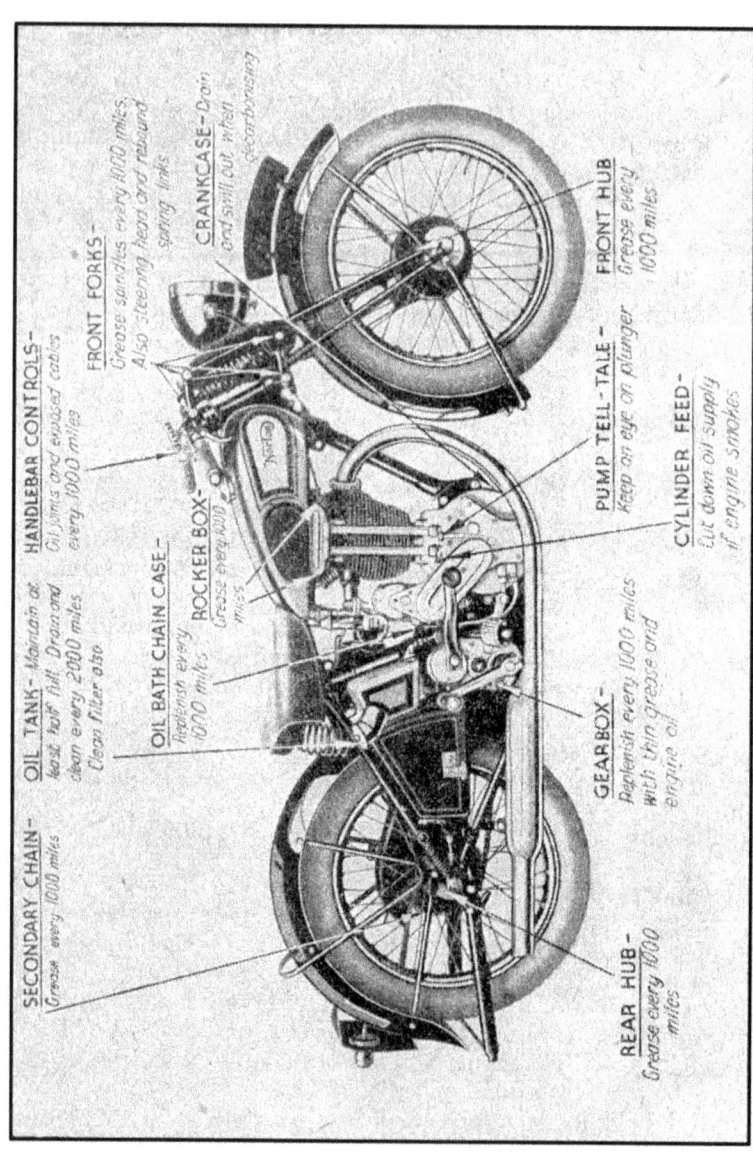

FIG. 29.

LUBRICATION CHART SHOWING WHEN AND WHERE TO LUBRICATE

The above chart, illustrating a fully-equipped 1936–7 Model 18 Norton, is applicable in general to the whole Norton range, but is intended as a guide rather than to be scrupulously complied with. In the case of the 1936-7 side-valve models, grease the valve guide nipples every 800–1000 miles. On the overhead camshaft machines and 1938 and later O.H.V.s the rocker-box is automatically lubricated. On 1938 and later models there is no adjustable cylinder feed (except O.H.C.) and no oil indicator

LUBRICATION

chain, although plain engine oil or regular greasing will answer satisfactorily. On 1935 and later Nortons the secondary chain is automatically lubricated by oil mist from the crankcase breather, but it requires greasing about every 1000 miles and the treatment described on page 47 is recommended.

The " Magdyno " Chain. On all Nortons the chain requires no attention and is automatically lubricated.

Fork Spindles and Steering Head. Both the ball bearings in the steering head and the fork-link spindles require periodic lubrication. Grease-gun lubrication nipples are provided, and the gun should be applied about every 1000–1500 miles. On 1934 and later models, lubricate the links of the fork rebound springs. Wakefield's "Castrolease Medium," Shell Retinax, or Price's Belmoline is suitable for here. (See also page 102.)

Wheel Hubs. On both front and rear wheels, nipples are provided, and the hubs should be charged with one egg-cupful of grease every 1000–1500 miles. Do not use excessive grease or it may get on the brake linings. Where a sidecar is fitted, do not neglect to lubricate the sidecar hub. It is exceedingly important to keep the bearings of all wheels well greased, as they are called upon to perform much heavy work, but do not inject excessive grease because it may get on the brake linings.

Brakes. The brake fulcrum pins, pedal shaft, and brake joints should be given a greasing regularly, say, every 1000–1500 miles. Grease nipples are provided on all recent models.

Control Levers. It will forestall the time when the Bowden control cables snap if a certain amount of oil or grease be periodically applied (1000 miles) where they are apt to bind on the control mechanism on the handlebars. When fitting new cables and casings, the latter should be charged with grease. A piece of rubber tubing and a grease-gun will assist. Oil all control pins.

Use Colloidal Graphite During Running-in. The Norton Motors, Ltd. recommend the mixing of Colloidal Graphite with the oil during the running-in period in the proportions of 1 pint to each gallon of oil.

Spring Frame Lubrication, etc. Every 1000 miles some grease should be injected into the nipples in the fork ends. Grease the speedometer drive and oil saddle pin every 2000 miles.

CHAPTER V

LUCAS ELECTRIC-LIGHTING EQUIPMENT

INSTRUCTIONS for the maintenance of the magneto unit of the "Magdyno" will be found on page 64. In this chapter we are concerned with the dynamo portion alone, together with the lamps and battery. The following instructions apply to the electric lighting equipment used on 1932 and later Nortons.

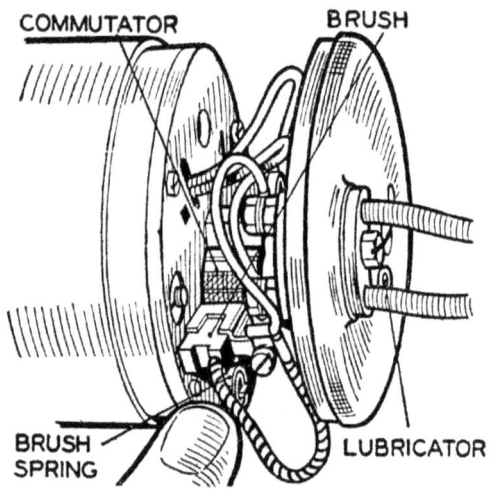

FIG. 30. COMMUTATOR END OF DYNAMO PORTION OF THE 1937–47 "MAGDYNO"

Some thin machine oil should be put in the lubricator (where fitted) about every 4000–5000 miles.

DYNAMO MAINTENANCE

Before removing the cover for any reason, it is necessary to disconnect the positive lead at the battery to avoid the danger of reversing the polarity of the dynamo or short-circuiting the battery, either of which might cause serious damage. To disconnect, move the rubber shield and unscrew the cable connector, being careful not to touch the frame with the cable and cause a short circuit. When reconnecting, make sure the rubber shield is pulled well over the connector.

If at any time the motor-cycle must be ridden with the battery

LUCAS ELECTRIC-LIGHTING EQUIPMENT

disconnected, or in any way out of service, it is essential to run with the switch in the "OFF" position (automatic voltage control excepted).

Brushes. It is very important to make sure that the brushes

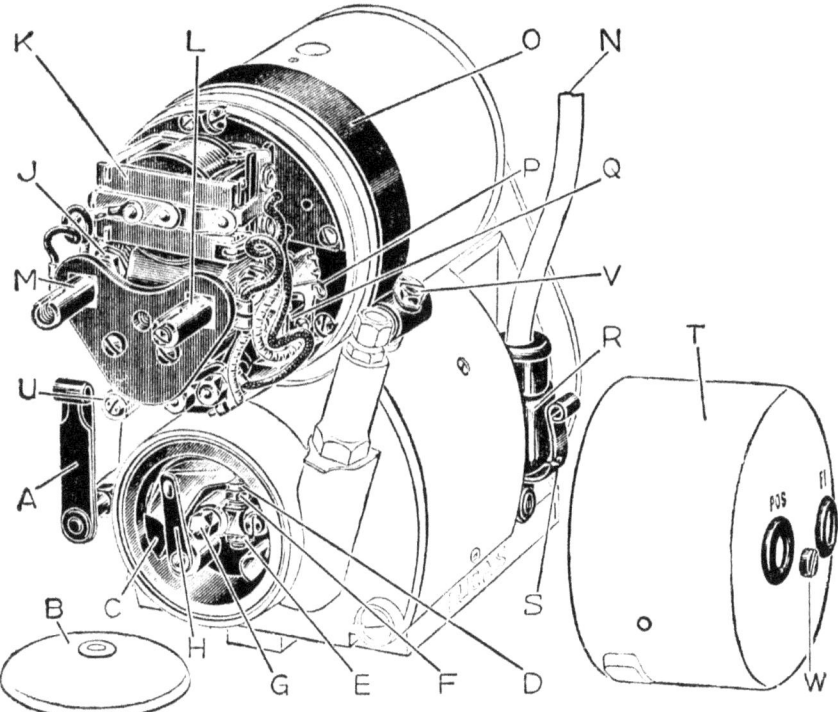

FIG. 30A. 1935–6 LUCAS "MAGDYNO" WITH CUT-OUT

A = Securing spring for contact breaker cover
B = Contact breaker cover
C = Fibre heel
D = Contact points
E = Locking nut
F = Adjustable contact point
G = Contact breaker fixing screw
H = Locating spring
J = Nut securing brush eyelet
K = Cut-out
L = Terminal marked "F1"
M = Terminal marked "POS"
N = Cable to sparking plug
O = Dynamo securing strap
P = Spring lever holding brush in position
Q = Carbon brush
R = Pick-up
S = Securing spring for pick-up
T = Cover
U = Earthing terminal
V = Screw securing dynamo strap
W = Cover fixing screw

work freely in their holders. This can be easily ascertained by holding back the spring lever and gently pulling each flexible lead, when the brush should move without the slightest suggestion of sluggishness. It should also return to its original position directly the lead is let go. When testing the brush in this way, release it gently, otherwise it may get chipped. The brushes should be clean and "bed" over the whole surface; that is, the face in contact with the commutator should appear uniformly polished. Dirty brushes may be cleaned with a cloth moistened with petrol.

If the brushes become so badly worn that it is necessary to remove them, this can easily be done as follows: Release the eyelet on the brush lead by unscrewing the hexagonal nut or screw at the terminal; then, holding back the spring lever out of the way, withdraw the brush from its holder. Replace with genuine Lucas brushes.

The brush springs should be inspected occasionally to see that they have sufficient tension to keep the brushes firmly pressed against the commutator when the machine is running. It is particularly necessary to keep this in mind when the brushes have been in use a long time and are very much worn down. Owners are cautioned that it is unwise to insert brushes of a grade other than that supplied with the machine, or to change the tension springs. The arrangement provided has been made only after many years' experience, and will be found to give the best results and the longest life. It is really best when the brushes become so worn that they no longer bed down on the commutator, to go to a Lucas Service Depot, as this ensures the brushes being properly "bedded."

Commutator. The surface of the commutator should be kept clean and free from oil or brush dust, etc. Should any grease or oil work its way on to the commutator through over-lubrication, it will not only cause sparking, but, in addition, carbon and copper dust will be collected in the grooves between the commutator segments. The best way to clean the commutator is, without disconnecting any leads, to remove from its box one of the main brushes and, inserting a fine duster in the box, hold it, by means of a suitably-shaped piece of wood, against the commutator surface, causing the armature to be rotated at the same time. If the commutator has been neglected for long periods, it may need cleaning with fine glasspaper, but this is more difficult to do, and should not be necessary if it has received regular attention.

Terminals. The positive dynamo terminal, marked "POS", and the shunt-field terminal, marked "FI", are situated on either side of the cover (Fig. 30A). To connect up, the cables merely have to be bared and clamped in their terminals by means of grub screws.

On the Lucas "Magdyno" (Fig. 30) with separate voltage control unit the positive dynamo terminal is marked "D" and the shunt-field terminal "F" on the cover. To connect up, first slacken the fixing screw on the terminal block and remove the clamping plate. Then withdraw the metal sleeve from each terminal. The cables should then be passed through the clamping plate holes and bared at the ends for ⅜ in. Now fit the sleeves over the cables, bend back the wires over them and push the sleeves home into the terminals, finally screwing down the clamping plate.

Electro-magnetic Cut-out. The cut-out automatically closes the charging circuit by means of solenoids, as soon as the dynamo voltage rises above that of the battery. When the dynamo voltage falls below that of the battery, the reverse action takes place, that is, the cut-out opens and thereby prevents the battery from discharging itself through the dynamo. Leave cut-out alone.

The cut-out is accurately set before leaving the Works.

Absence of Fuses. In order to simplify the system as far as possible, no fuse is provided. If all the connections are kept clean and tight, there is no possibility of any excess current causing damage to the equipment.

Ammeter. This gives a reading of the amount of current flowing into or from the battery and shows whether the equipment is functioning satisfactorily. It is of the centre-zero type.

CARE OF THE BATTERY (LEAD-ACID TYPE)

It is of the utmost importance that the battery should receive regular attention to keep it in good condition.

The following are the most important maintenance hints—
1. Keep the acid level to the top of the separators.
2. Add only distilled water, never tap water.
3. Test the condition of the battery by taking readings of the specific gravity of the acid with a hydrometer.
4. The battery must never be left in a discharged condition.

Topping-up. At least once a month the filler caps on top of the battery should be removed and the level of the acid solution examined. If necessary, distilled water, which can be obtained at all chemists and most garages, should be added to bring the level to the top of the separators. Replenish with a suitable small syringe. If, however, acid solution has been spilled, it should be replaced by diluted sulphuric acid solution of the same specific gravity. It is important when examining the cells that naked lights should not be held near the vents, on account of the possible danger of igniting the gas coming from the plates. At monthly intervals or if acid has been spilled, test the specific gravity with a hydrometer (S.G. 1·280-1·300, fully charged).

Storage. If the equipment is laid by for several months, the battery must be given a small charge from a separate source of electrical energy about once a fortnight, in order to obviate any permanent sulphation of the plates. In no circumstances must the electrolyte be removed from the battery and the plates allowed to dry, as certain chemical changes take place which result in permanent loss of capacity.

Battery-charging (1932-6). It is difficult to lay down rigid instructions on this subject, as the conditions under which motor-cycles are used vary considerably; and, obviously, the amount of charging a battery will require is directly dependent on the current used. The following suggestions will serve as a rough guide where automatic voltage control is not fitted.

The switch should be left in the C position for about 1 hour daily. This time should only be increased if the period of night running is considerable, or when the battery is found to be in a low state of charge (if the specific gravity of the acid solution is 1·210 or below). Where a sidecar is fitted and/or an electric horn, considerably more charging is necessary. Overcharging will cause nothing worse than loss of acid by gassing, but undercharging may spoil the battery by causing sulphation of the plates.

The battery must never be left fully discharged (S.G. below 1·150). Unless some long runs are to be taken, it is advisable to have the battery removed from the machine and charged up from an independent electrical supply.

LAMPS

The DU142 Headlamp. This lamp, used on all recent Nortons where no instrument panel is provided, is fitted with a double filament bulb, the one filament providing the normal driving light, while the second one gives an anti-dazzle dipped beam. The change over from the normal driving light to the dipped beam is made by a handlebar switch. A small pilot bulb is provided for use when the machine is stationary or when driving in town.

An ammeter is incorporated in the lamp, which gives the driver an indication of the amount of current in amperes by which the battery is being charged or discharged under the various conditions governed by the particular position of the switch. When the lamp is switched on, the ammeter is illuminated by indirect lighting. This is arranged by means of two small apertures situated in the reflector, from which light is reflected across the dial through slots in the ammeter case. A special mask is placed across the ammeter dial to prevent any glare that would tend to distract the rider's attention from the road.

LUCAS ELECTRIC-LIGHTING EQUIPMENT

The D142 Headlamp. This headlamp is used on all Nortons with an instrument panel and is very similar to the DU142 headlamp, but it contains neither switch nor ammeter, these being housed in the instrument panel. As with the DU142 headlamp, a double filament bulb is used, one filament (for normal driving light) being placed at the focus of the reflector, and the other (for

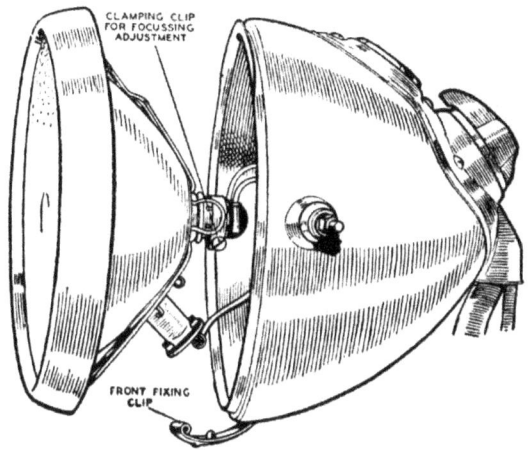

Fig. 31. Lucas DU142 Headlamp Used on Most Models

dipped beam) being situated slightly above it. A small pilot bulb is also incorporated for parking purposes and when driving in well illuminated streets. The panel switch positions are the same.

Switch Positions. The lighting switch housed on the back of the lamp or instrument panel has the following positions—
"Off"—Lamps off, and dynamo not charging.
C—Lamps off and dynamo giving half its normal output.
H—Headlamp (driving light), tail lamp, and sidecar lamp (when fitted) on; dynamo giving maximum output (4-5 amp.)
L—With the exception that the pilot light is in the place of the driving light, the conditions are exactly the same as in position H. For 1937 and later models the "C" position is omitted (page 59).

Focusing H52 Headlamp. To ensure that the main bulb filament is approximately at the focus of the reflector, the bulb-holder is arranged so that it can be adjusted. By turning the bulb in a clockwise direction it is moved inwards, and by turning it in an anti-clockwise direction it is moved outwards. The best position can readily be found by trial. The normal driving light should, of course, be switched on while focusing is being carried out.

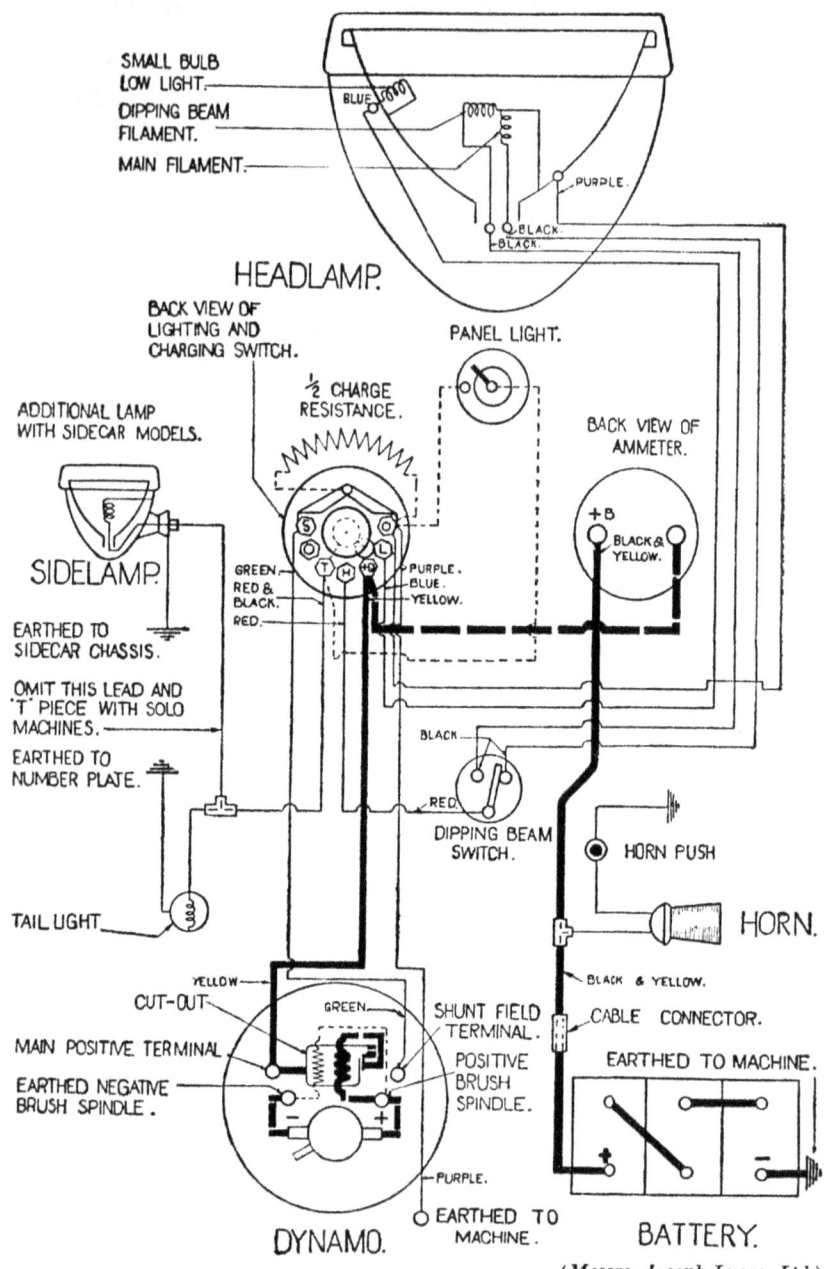

Fig. 32. Wiring Diagram for the Lucas "Magdyno" Lighting Equipment with D142 Headlamp
This W.D. applies to 1936 and earlier Nortons with instrument panel but without compensated voltage control.

LUCAS ELECTRIC-LIGHTING EQUIPMENT

In adjusting the bulb, it is important that it is given a complete turn at a time, so that the filaments are in the correct position; a spring stop is incorporated in the holder, which indicates every time the bulb has been given a complete turn by a click action.

The best way of focusing and setting the lamp is to take the motor-cycle to a straight, level road; find the correct bulb adjustment; and then move the lamp on its adjustable mounting until the best road position is obtained.

Focusing DU142 and D142 Headlamps. On machines with or without an instrument panel the focusing of the headlamp is carried out in the same manner. To focus the main bulb it is necessary to remove the lamp front and reflector by pressing back the fixing clip. Then slacken the clamping screw which secures the bulb-holder and move the bulb-holder and bulb until correct focus is obtained. Afterwards tighten the clamping screw. To remove the bulb-holder it is only necessary to press back the two securing springs. When replacing the lamp front and reflector the top of the rim should be located first.

Sidecar Lamp (Type LD309). To remove the lamp front and reflector twist the front to the left, and withdraw. The bulb-holder can then be unclipped from the back of the reflector. When replacing, push the front on so that the arrow stamped on the rim is slightly to the left of the top, and then turn the front until the arrow is at the top of the lamp.

Sidecar Lamp (Type R370). By unscrewing the locating screw at the bottom of the rim, the lamp front and reflector may be removed. The top of the rim should be located first when replacing.

Tail Lamp (MT110). This lamp is mounted directly on the number plate; it displays a red light to the rear, and through the side window illuminates the number plate.

The bulb-holder is mounted on a rubber diaphragm, which prevents road and engine vibration from being transmitted to the filament, thus greatly prolonging its life.

The rear portion of the lamp is removed for bulb replacements by giving it a half-turn to the left, when it becomes detached from its bayonet fixing.

Replacement of Bulbs. When the replacement of any bulb is necessary, genuine Lucas bulbs should be used. The filaments are arranged to be in focus, and give the best results with Lucas reflectors. When it is found necessary to replace the main headlamp bulb, screw it out two or three turns in an anti-clockwise direction. This will release the pressure on the bulb contacts and

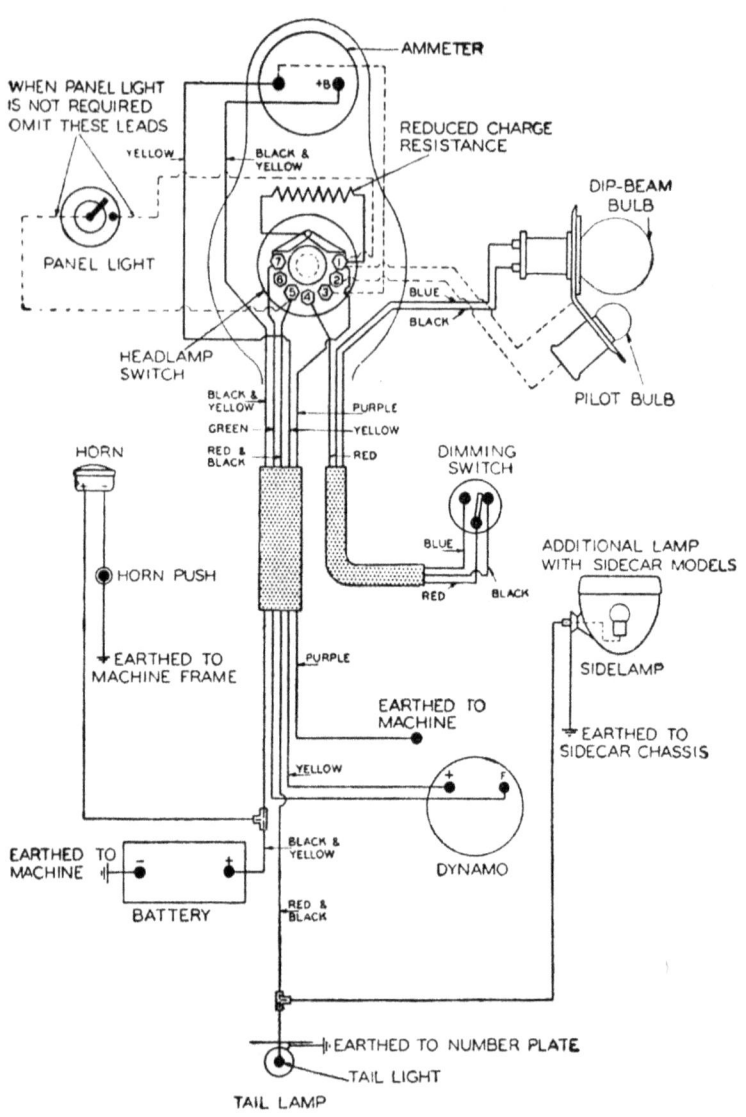

(*Joseph Lucas, Ltd.*)

FIG. 33. WIRING DIAGRAM FOR LUCAS "MAGDYNO" LIGHTING EQUIPMENT WITH DU142 HEADLAMP

All internal connections are shown dotted and the W.D. applies to 1936 and earlier Nortons without instrument panel and without compensated voltage control.

LUCAS ELECTRIC-LIGHTING EQUIPMENT

enable the bulb to be withdrawn easily. Care should be taken that the bulb is fitted the correct way round, i.e. with the dipped beam filament above the centre filament. Always focus the headlamp after fitting a new bulb.

The number of the bulb for the headlamp driving and dipped beam light is 70; and that of the headlamp pilot, side-car, panel, and tail lights, 200. These two bulbs are of the gas-filled and centre contact type respectively.

WIRING OF THE EQUIPMENT

Before making any alteration to the wiring, or removing the switch from the back of the headlamp or panel, disconnect the positive lead at the battery to prevent the possibility of short circuits.

All cables to the headlamp are taken directly into the switch, which can be easily withdrawn from the lamp body when the three fixing screws are removed.

The ends of all the cables are identified by means of coloured sleevings as shown on the wiring diagrams. When making a connection, proceed as follows: bare about $\frac{3}{8}$ in. of the cable, twist the wire strands together, and turn back about $\frac{1}{8}$ in. so as to form a small ball. Remove the grub screw from the appropriate terminal and insert the wire so that the ball fits in the terminal post. Now replace and tighten the grub screw; this will compress the ball to make a good electrical connection.

Compensated Voltage Control. This is used on post-1936 Nortons, and a wiring diagram is given on page 135. The control unit comprises the cut-out and voltage control (working on the trembler principle) neatly housed in a box on the off-side near the saddle. It sees to it that the battery is kept properly charged automatically, the dynamo output varying according to the state of charge of the battery and the load. With this equipment the switch resistance is omitted and there are only three positions—"Off," "L," and "H" for the switch. In all three positions the dynamo gives a controlled output, thus relieving the rider of much responsibility. During daylight running when the battery is well charged the ammeter may indicate a charge of only 1 or 2 amperes, for the dynamo gives only a trickle charge. The voltage control unit is sealed by the makers and should not be tampered with, the only likely trouble being oxidizing or welding together of the contacts due to accidental crossing of the dynamo field and positive leads. If a "Nife" battery is fitted, the regulator should be changed at a Lucas service depot. Excellent service is given at Lucas depots and the reader is advised to call at one whenever any spot of bother is encountered in regard to the electrical equipment.

CHAPTER VI
ADJUSTMENTS AND OVERHAULING

IT should be particularly noted that the whole of the information given in this chapter applies to 1932-47 models except where otherwise stated.

There is a number of minor adjustments which it is desirable that the Norton rider should attend to every few hundred miles.

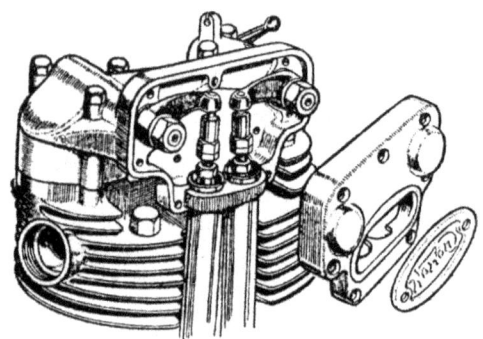

(From "The Motor Cycle")

FIG. 34. THE PUSH-ROD ADJUSTMENT ON 1938-47 NORTONS

Adjusters are provided at the upper ends of the push-rods and the valve clearance should be such that, with the engine cold, the push-rods may be freely revolved without up-and-down motion.

Cleaning. It requires a considerable amount of time to keep a motor-cycle in anything approaching "showroom" condition, but it is the author's opinion that, unless a machine be kept reasonably clean, the fullest pleasure and maximum efficiency cannot be obtained from it. Apart from the question of pride of ownership (and the present range is very handsome indeed with the enamel and chromium plating unsoiled), it is an undoubted fact that dirt covers a multitude of defects and greatly accelerates depreciation in respect of market value. This is, of course, obvious. If neglected, a motor-cycle rapidly becomes shabby and an eyesore. After a ride in dirty weather, cleaning may take at least an hour. It entails the use of stiff bristle brushes and paraffin for removing the filth from the lower extremities, together with cloths, leather, and polish for the enamelled parts. On no account should a machine be left soaking wet overnight. A serious

ADJUSTMENTS AND OVERHAULING

amount of rusting may ensue. If the rider is so preoccupied that he cannot spare the necessary time for cleaning, the machine should be thoroughly greased all over before use.

It should be noted that chromium plating does not require and should not be treated with metal polish, for it does not oxidize in the same manner as nickel plating. The chromium-plated parts should be treated with leather cloths only, and the surfaces will then improve with cleaning.

Valve Clearances. In order that the valves shall seat properly and have the correct degree of lift at normal running temperature, it is extremely important that the correct clearances should exist when the engine is *cold* between the valve stems and the tappet heads, or rocker studs, as the case may be, according to whether the engine be of S.V. or O.H.V. type. The clearances (except on 1938-47 O.H.V.s) should be checked now and again with the feeler gauge on the magneto spanner, although it is unlikely that adjustment will be needed, unless a big mileage has been completed, or the engine is new or the valves have been ground-in. The clearances for the exhaust valves, it will be noted, are larger than the inlet valve clearances, due to the fact that the exhaust valve operates at a higher temperature and, therefore, expands to a greater extent than the inlet valve. (See also page 102.)

VALVE CLEARANCES RECOMMENDED
(Engine Cold)

Engine (see page 103)	Inlet Valve	Exhaust Valve
S.V. (1932-47)	·004 in.	·006 in.
O.H.V. Push-rod (1932-37)	·002 in.	·004 in.
O.H.V. Push-rod (1938-47)	Nil	Nil
O.H.C. (1932-9)	·008 in.	·012 in.
O.H.C. (1932-9) Racing	·012 in.	·020 in.
O.H.C. ("Internationals")	·010 in.	·020 in.

To check and adjust the clearance at the exhaust valve, proceed as follows: Turn the engine over until compression is felt after the inlet valve has just closed, and then raise the exhaust valve-lifter a trifle, and further rotate the engine until the piston is at the top of its stroke and both valves are closed. See that the exhaust valve-lifter is in no way determining the clearance. There should be an appreciable interval between the moment when the lifter is raised and the exhaust valve is lifted off its seat.

Then insert a feeler gauge of the correct dimension between the tappet head and the base of the valve stem, or between the ball-ended rocker grub-screw (Fig. 34A) and the stem, on 1932-7 O.H.V.s. It should just go in without binding. If the clearances are found to be incorrect, they must at once be rectified. To do this, loosen the lock-nut (see Figs. 34, 34A) and, according to

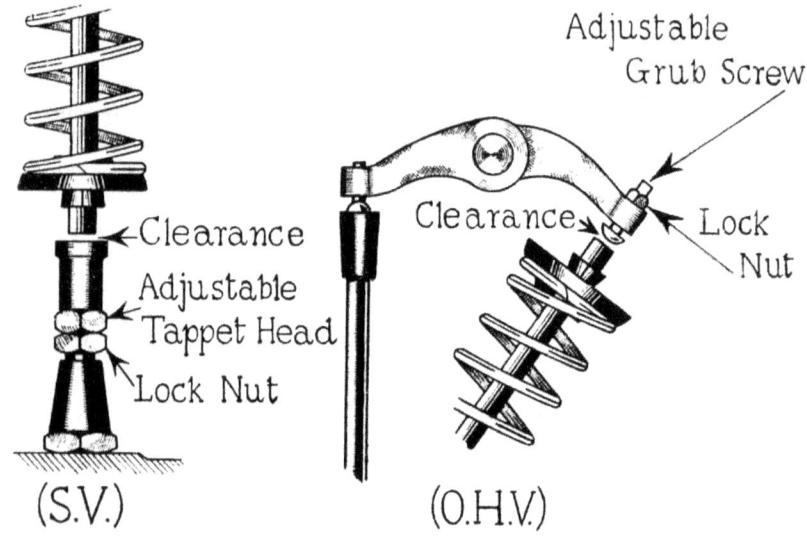

FIG. 34A. SHOWING VALVE CLEARANCE ADJUSTMENT ON 1932-7 S.V. AND 1932-7 O.H.V. NORTON ENGINES

On the O.H.C. models (CSI, CJ, 30, 40) the valve clearance adjustment is different from that on the O.H.V. engines (see Fig. 35).

whether it is necessary to increase or decrease the clearance, screw up or unscrew the tappet head or grub-screw. Finally retighten the lock-nut and once again check the clearance. On 1938-47 O.H.V. engines the push-rods must be able to revolve freely. Proceed similarly with the inlet valve clearance adjustment. The adjustment of the overhead valves described above does not apply in the case of the overhead camshaft engines. Here ball-ended grub-screws and lock-nuts are not used. Instead a pad (see Fig. 35) is secured by a lock-nut in a sleeve screwed into the rocker-arm. To adjust the valve clearance, slacken the lock-nut to free the pad from the sleeve and then screw out or in the sleeve by means of the hexagon head below the pad lock-nut. Before checking the valve clearance tighten the lock-nut which holds the pad firmly in the sleeve.

Exhaust Valve-lifter Adjustment. As already mentioned, it is

ADJUSTMENTS AND OVERHAULING

important that there should not be an entire absence of backlash at the exhaust valve-lifter lever, which would inevitably prevent the exhaust valve from seating properly, and thus cause loss of compression and burning of the valve and its seating, accompanied by intermittent banging in the exhaust pipe and silencer. There should be about $\frac{1}{16}$ in. backlash at the handlebar control,

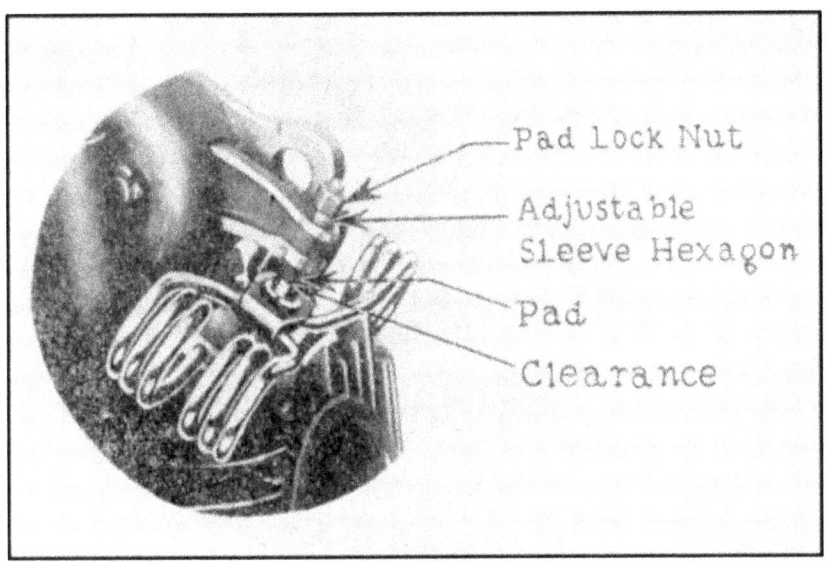

FIG. 35. THE VALVE CLEARANCE ADJUSTMENT ON THE O.H.C. MODELS

and the desired adjustment may be effected by means of the adjustable cable stop placed, in the case of the S.V. engine, close by the exhaust port, and on the near side of the rocker-box on the O.H.V. and O.H.C. engines.

The Sparking Plug. Difficult starting or occasional misfiring can usually be traced to a dirty or defective sparking plug. The life of a good plug is considerable, but the points of the electrodes gradually burn away and eventually the gap becomes enlarged considerably, and it is necessary to reset the points with the aid of a feeler gauge.

The correct plug gap is ·015–·018 in. Excessive gap at the plug means that voltage required from the "Magdyno" is higher; and this not only renders starting difficult, but—what is worse—causes brush discharge inside the "Magdyno." This discharge eventually causes internal corrosion, and efficiency of the "Magdyno" is impaired. From time to time the plug should be dismantled, thoroughly cleaned with petrol, both inside and outside. All deposits of soot or charred oil must be eliminated, as these are apt to cause leakage and bad running. The insulation should be examined for cracks or flaws, and in very humid weather should be wiped dry with a rag before starting-up. The accepted method

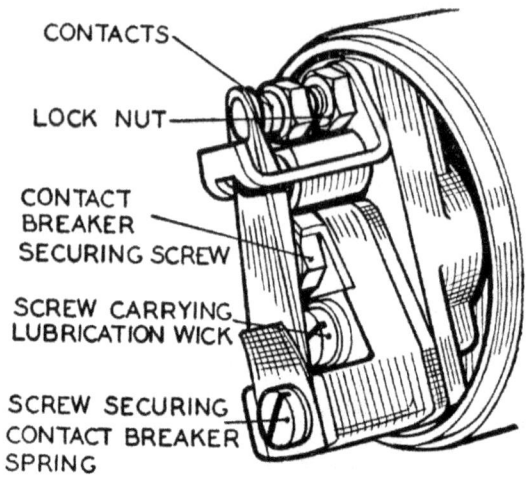

FIG. 36. LUCAS FACE CAM CONTACT-BREAKER

Most recent "Magdynos" have this contact-breaker, but some have the older ring cam type (Figs. 30A, 48).

of testing for current at the plug terminal is to place a wooden-handled screw-driver, with steel blade, across the terminal and just touching the cylinder fin, when a spark should be visible on rotating the engine. To test the plug itself, remove it with the H.T. lead still affixed, clean it, lay it on the cylinder, and note whether it sparks satisfactorily when the engine is rotated. If it does not, scrap it. Always fit the correct type of plug recommended by the manufacturers. (See page 25.)

The Contact-breaker. The magneto portion of the "Magdyno" or the magneto should not be interfered with unnecessarily, and functions best when left well alone; but at regular intervals, say every 1000 miles, the contact-breaker cover should be removed and the contacts (see Figs. 30A, 36, and 36A) should be examined, and their gap checked with a ·010–·012 feeler gauge. If the clearance is excessive, the timing will be advanced and the primary circuit will not be closed for the correct period, and occasional misfiring is very likely. Provided the contacts are kept clean and, above all, *free from oil*, they will probably need adjustment

ADJUSTMENTS AND OVERHAULING

only at long intervals. It is not desirable to alter the setting unless the gap varies considerably from that of the magneto spanner gauge. If adjustment is necessary, rotate the engine round slowly until the points are seen to be fully opened and then, using the magneto spanner, slacken the lock-nut and rotate the fixed contact screw by its hexagonal head until the correct gap is obtained, as indicated by the feeler gauge; then screw up the lock-nut firmly.

If, when the contact points are examined, it is found that they have become burned or blackened (owing probably to the presence at some time or other of dirt or oil), they may be cleaned with very fine emery cloth, and afterwards with a cloth damped with petrol. All dirt and metal dust must be wiped away entirely. Where the contacts are found to have become seriously pitted, it will be advisable to true up the surfaces with a fine carborundum stone and only the very smallest amount of metal must be removed. Removing the contact-breaker unit will be necessary for this purpose. Instructions for removing the contact-breaker rocker-arm or spring will be found on page 85, and advice on timing the "break" on page 88.

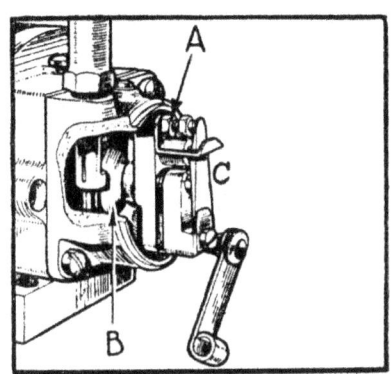

FIG. 36A. CONTACT-BREAKER MECHANISM ON THE M-L MAGNETO

At A, B, C, are shown the contacts, face cam, and contact-breaker spring respectively.

Any sign of incipient rusting on the contact-breaker spring should be checked immediately, as rust and corrosion are frequent causes of broken contact-breaker springs.

In the case of the M-L contact-breaker, it is as well occasionally to examine the plunger and also the control spring, and to grease these thoroughly, as any rusting here may possibly cause binding of the control and sticking of the tappet in its guide.

Clutch Adjustment. Nothing is more exasperating or inconvenient on a motor-cycle than clutch-slip. The cable adjustment should be adjusted until there is approximately $\frac{1}{8}$ in. of idle movement at the end of the clutch-worm lever. It may be necessary to loosen the clutch-worm lever from the worm to find a more convenient operating position. The only parts of the clutch liable to wear are the friction plates, which are easily replaced. The clutch should be adjusted immediately any sign of slipping is felt.

Should oil get on a 1932-3 clutch, as may occur when newly assembled, this will cause slipping; to overcome, inject petrol. A sure sign of slipping is given by the clutch becoming very warm whilst driving. On 1934 and later oil bath models oil is not likely to cause the Ferodo-lined plates to slip. (See also page 117.)

When fitting up the control wire for the clutch, ease off the bends as much as possible to ensure long life and easy movement of the inner wire, and keep the cable greased where friction

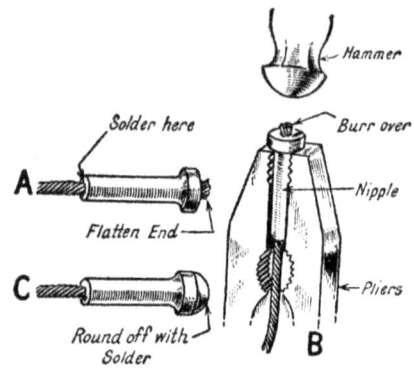

FIG. 37. HOW A NIPPLE SHOULD BE SOLDERED
A nipple should be soldered on to a Bowden cable as shown in the order A, B, C.

occurs. Lack of free movement in the clutch worm lever (equivalent to ½ in. to ¾ in. at the handlebar lever) with the Bowden cable slackened off at the cable stop may be caused through the shoulder on the worm bearing on the face of the felt washer, this washer being held in place by a steel cap on which are machined two flats to take a spanner. The remedy is to release the steel cap a few threads. Always keep the clutch spring boxes done up tightly.

Gear-control Adjustment (Hand Type Control). Whenever primary chain adjustment is carried out on early machines with hand control, there is the risk of upsetting the control. It is most important that the gear control is kept properly adjusted, and this should be tested occasionally to see that it is correct. Before actually proceeding to adjust the control, see that the nut of the rocking shaft behind the box is tight. The adjustment of the gear is effected by removing the pin from the bottom connection on the end of the control rod, and giving the connection half a turn on the thread up or down to lengthen or shorten the control rod as required. When the gear is properly adjusted, the control lever should move an *equal* amount either side of the neutral notch without engaging either the second or low gears. Finally check

ADJUSTMENTS AND OVERHAULING

by the pin in the connection being just free to slide with the pressure of the thumb and finger when in top gear. If the gear control is mounted directly on the box, no adjustments will, of course, be required. A jerky or slipping middle gear is usually due to faulty control adjustment, but may possibly be caused by

FIG. 38. SHOWING THE REAR BRAKE ANCHOR PLATE WITH SHOES IN POSITION AND THE QUICKLY-DETACHABLE WHEEL HUB

The dust cover provided on the 1935 models has been omitted for 1938-47. Note how the hub has been lightened and provided with an exposed wheel fixing bolt.

worn dogs. The same remark applies in respect of a nasty tendency for jumping out of low gear.

Adjusting the Brakes. If the brakes are used frequently and heavily, the friction linings are apt to wear, and adjustment becomes necessary.

In the case of the rear internal expanding brake (see Fig. 38), there are two separate adjustments.

In addition to provision for taking up lining wear, an independent adjustment is provided for altering the angle of the brake pedal pad, so that in all positions of the adjustable footrests the brake can be conveniently operated without removing the foot from the rests. The wing nut (A, Fig. 38A) at the extreme end of the brake rod should be turned in a clockwise direction to take up wear. To alter the angle of the pad, proceed as follows: slack off the wing-nut, loosen the brake pedal stop lock-nut (B, Fig. 38A), and adjust the hexagon-headed stop screw to give the required position of the pedal; tighten the lock-nut and then the wing-nut until the brake is correctly adjusted. When adjusting the wing-nut, place the gear lever in neutral and tighten the wing-nut until the minimum amount of pedal movement operates the brake without, however, any suspicion of friction when the pedal is released and the wheel is rotated by hand.

Adjustment of the operating mechanism of the front brake is

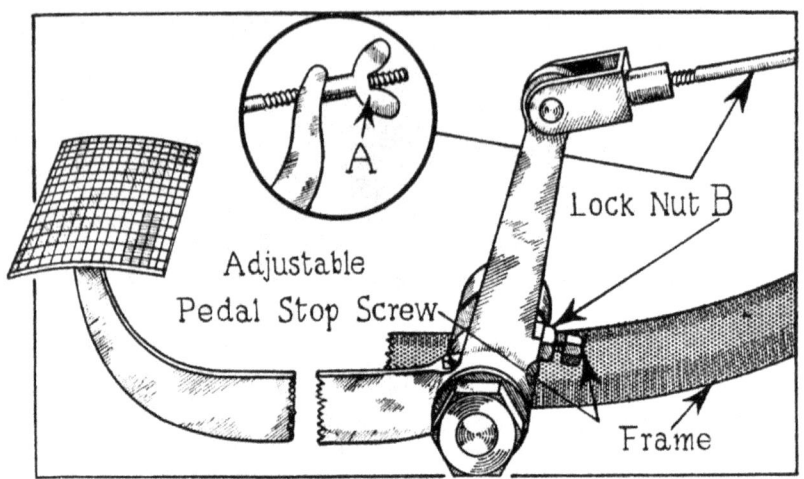

Fig. 38a. The Dual Adjustment for the Rear Brake
Comprising an adjustable pedal stop and a wing-nut A for adjusting the length of the brake-rod.

provided on the Bowden wire adjuster, which is fitted in a lug brazed to the forks. To adjust on the 1932–8 models, grip the adjuster with a small fixed spanner; and to take up wear of the control cable and friction linings, rotate in an anti-clockwise direction after first loosening the lock-nut. After adjustment, re-tighten this nut. On all later models finger adjustment is provided and the shoes should be made to come as close to the drums as possible without causing friction when the brake is off.

If either brake is harsh in action or tends to squeak, remove the anchor plate (see Fig. 38) and file each lining thin for about 1 in. from each end. This slightly reduces the effective area of the brake lining but results in much smoother braking without any appreciable decrease in efficiency. Smooth hard linings should be roughened up with a file and oily ones cleaned with petrol.

Tyres. Check the tyre inflation pressures (see page 22) about once a week and, if found low, pump up to the requisite lbs. per square inch by a tyre gauge. Never run for even a brief interval with the rear tyre deflated, as the fabric of the cover, as well as the inner tube, suffer severely if this is done, and the damage may be almost irreparable. From time to time inspect the covers with the machine jacked up, and remove all small flints with a sharp penknife. This practice often saves a hold-up on the road, as flints which get embedded in the rubber usually penetrate deeper as the machine is continued to be run. Never leave the machine standing for days on end unjacked, as this is bad for both wheels and tyres. Also avoid letting the machine stand in a welter of oil or paraffin, which causes tyres to soften and deteriorate very rapidly. With regard to tyre pressures, if a gauge is not at hand an approximately correct pressure can be obtained by pumping up the tyres until when astride the machine all the rows of studs make contact with the ground. Always carry an efficient tyre repair outfit, and do not mend punctures hastily with poor material, as if this is done the tubes quickly lose their air-retaining properties. (See page 122.)

Handlebar Adjustment. Nearly all Norton machines have handlebars which may be readily adjusted for reach by undoing two nuts, but no attempt should be made to adjust the angle of the 1935–9 insulated handlebars.

The Primary Chain. Since this is automatically lubricated or totally enclosed in an oil bath chain case, stretching takes considerably longer than is the case with the secondary chain, which is much more exposed to harmful influences. However, it will stretch in time, and it must be retensioned correctly. If a chain is too slack, it is apt to "whip," which intensifies the wear and tends to break the rollers, especially in the case of the front chain. On the other hand, if it be too tight, a crushing stress is produced on the rollers, and the whole chain is subjected to unfair stresses, and the sprockets wear quickly. The chain should be adjusted and kept adjusted, so that it can be given midway by pressure with the fingers a total and maximum deflection of $\frac{3}{8}$ in. to $\frac{1}{2}$ in. Adjustment is effected by slackening the top and bottom gear-box bolt nuts, and turning the adjuster passing through the upper gearbox lug and the bolt clockwise until the correct tension is arrived at. After making an adjustment, see that the gear control (if hand type) has not been upset and, if it has, adjust as described on page 66. Also retighten the two gearbox bolt nuts.

The Secondary Chain. The secondary chain requires to be tensioned at regular intervals, depending upon the mileage of the machine and how the rider has lubricated the chain. (See page 47.) This chain should undergo a total maximum deflection of $\frac{1}{2}$ in. to $\frac{3}{4}$ in. when properly adjusted. To do this, unscrew the wing-nut on the rear brake rod, slightly loosen the two hub spindle nuts and unscrew the two spindle adjuster lock-nuts, being careful not to disturb the adjusters. Turn the adjuster screws so that each side is about an equal distance and the correct chain tension is obtained. Finally tighten up the spindle nuts and lock-nuts. See that wheel alinement is not put out when making the above adjustment and afterwards adjust the rear brake (page 67). Make whatever further adjustments are found necessary. A rough-and-ready method of testing a chain for wear is to hold a length between the hands and observe to what extent the chain will bend sideways.

Coupling-up Chains. It greatly simplifies chain replacement if the obvious precaution be taken of uniting the two ends behind the vertical diameter of the large sprocket, in which case the whole of the tension is resisted by the sprocket teeth, and it is unnecessary to stretch the chain by hand. When replacing the spring link, see that the closed end faces the direction of motion, for when rapidly accelerating the whip of the chain may cause the spring-fastening to pull off. Uncoupling of a secondary chain or jumping off the sprockets at high speed is a factor of considerable gravity, for centrifugal force would cause the chain to fly off and perhaps wreck the chain guard, and possibly get entangled in the machine with disastrous consequences.

Steering-head Adjustment. This should be such that it allows perfect freedom without up-and-down play. To test this, support the crankcase so that the front wheel clears the ground and slacken the steering damper. Correct adjustment of the head bearings is obtained when the handlebars turn freely without any play. Play in the steering head is liable to damage the ball races, and also causes a tendency for instability on grease, as does play in the wheel bearings. To confirm the existence of play, try and lift the front portion of the mudguard and note if movement occurs between the top of the head lug and the bottom of the fork clip. To take up play slacken the fork clip locking-bolt and tighten the nut above the steering column. (See also page 124.)

Fork Adjustment. There should be no end-play in the fork links. To adjust on Norton models, slacken nuts about half a turn and retighten lock-nut, afterwards checking to see that the fork is quite free. (See notes on page 118.)

Shock Absorbers. A knob adjuster enables the shock absorbers to be adjusted to meet all varying road conditions. The shock absorbers should always be in operation to a certain extent. A

ADJUSTMENTS AND OVERHAULING

star washer inside the knob prevents any tendency for vibration to upset the adjustment.

Steering Damper. Adjust this to suit road conditions. Experience quickly enables the best use to be made of this fitment which is an integral fitting with the forks.

No Adjustment for Wheel Bearings. No adjustment is necessary

FIG. 39. REMOVING QUICKLY-DETACHABLE REAR WHEEL

or provided for the journal-type bearings fitted to the wheel hubs of Norton models.

To Remove Quickly-detachable Rear Wheel. First of all withdraw the hub spindle, distance piece and, in the case of some models, the plated cover from the right-hand side of the machine. This cover is held in position by a concealed claw spring, and it is only necessary to grip the cover under the hands and afterwards proceed to pull it away from the hub. If it appears to be unduly tight, insert a screwdriver or any handy instrument between the cover and the hub in order to force the cover off the hub. Remove the three sleeve nuts which secure the hub to the brake drum. The wheel may now be withdrawn from the brake drum and readily detached, leaving the drum and chain sprocket. The rear of the mudguard is detachable. (See also page 130.)

To Remove Front Wheel. Disconnect the front brake cable "U" piece from the brake lever, slacken both spindle nuts and lift the wheel out. If it is desired to remove the brake drum, unscrew the three sleeve nuts which are identical to those used on the rear wheel. For post-war models see page 130.

To Remove Sidecar Wheel. In order to detach the sidecar wheel all that is necessary is to withdraw the hub spindle and lift the wheel out.

To Remove Wheel Bearings. Detach the locking ring on the off-side of the hub with a peg spanner or punch. Then tap out from the opposite side the inner sleeve on which the inside races of the bearings are fitted. After removing the off-side bearing, tap out the other one by means of a suitable drift.

Wheel Alinement. If heavy tyre wear and freedom from skidding are to be avoided, it is essential to keep the wheels in proper alinement relative to each other and relative to the frame. The screw adjusters at the chain stays should be adjusted evenly on both sides.

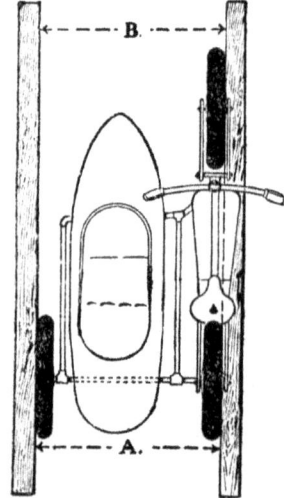

FIG. 40. SIDECAR ALINEMENT

The distance B should be $\frac{3}{4}$ in. less than the distance A.

When fitting or refitting a Norton sidecar, place the sidecar in position, leaving all attachment nuts slack. The sidecar wheel should not run parallel with the machine wheels, or there would be a tendency for the machine to constantly pull to the left. The sidecar wheel should run in towards the machine $\frac{3}{4}$ in. (See Fig. 40.) Alinement is regulated by the clip lug at the bottom of the centre sidecar arm, which can be moved along the cross tube of the chassis to which it is attached, and the clip lug of the rear arm which slides along the rear tube of the chassis. To aline correctly, two straight edges 6 ft. long are necessary, which should be placed on the floor, one against the wheel rims of the machine, the other against the wheel rims of the sidecar. Now measure the distance between the edges immediately in front of the front wheel and at the rear of the rear wheel, the distance between the edges should be $\frac{3}{4}$ in. less at the front than at the rear.

DECARBONIZING

After about 2000 miles have been covered, the accumulation of carbon deposits on the piston crown and in various parts of

ADJUSTMENTS AND OVERHAULING

the combustion chamber results in the engine losing its original "kick," and there is a marked decline in general all-round performance, accompanied by a tendency for knocking under the slightest provocation. In addition, the exhaust note becomes "woolly," and loses its virile crispness and low boom. When this happens it is a sure indication that the time has come for undertaking a "top overhaul," or, in other words, for decarbonizing and perhaps grinding-in the valves. Carbon deposits are inevitable on petrol engines, and are due to three things: (a) burnt lubricating oil; (b) carbonization of road dust; (c) incomplete fuel combustion. When decarbonizing it is always worth while inspecting the valve seatings and, *if necessary*, grinding-in the valves. Removal of the valves incidentally facilitates thorough cleaning of the ports.

In connection with decarbonization there are three types of engine to be taken account of: (a) the side-valve engine; (b) the overhead-valve engine; (c) the overhead-camshaft engine. The general procedure of decarbonizing is much the same in each case, although structural variations render the operations somewhat different. Never neglect decarbonizing for more than 3000 miles and do not grind-in the valves every time (see page 81).

The S.V. Engines. The S.V. type is perhaps the easiest to decarbonize, and involves simply the removal of the detachable cylinder head, unless it is desired to remove the piston when the cylinder barrel must also be removed complete with valves (although, if preferred, these may be removed first), after first removing the protective aluminium cover. Removal of the cylinder barrel on all Norton engines enables decarbonizing to be carried out more thoroughly.

The Overhead-valve Engines. All Norton O.H.V. engines have detachable cylinder heads, and it is unnecessary, unless it is desired to remove the piston or to inspect and remove the rings, to detach the cylinder barrel. In order to remove the cylinder head, however, it is necessary first to detach the push-rods complete with covers, and also the rocker-box, to allow of the head being lifted clear of the top cylinder barrel spigot.

The Overhead Camshaft Engines. Decarbonizing the O.H.C. type of engine is very similar to decarbonizing the ordinary pushrod operated O.H.V. type. It is necessary to remove the rocker-box after disconnecting the vertical shaft cover tube and then remove the cylinder head and barrel.

Initial Preparations. Jack the machine upon its stand and get out the tool kit. If the engine exterior is very dirty, go over it with a rag damped in paraffin, taking special care to clean the parts about to be dismantled, and see that a clean box or other receptacle is at hand in which to place the various parts prior to reassembly. Put the engine on compression and begin stripping the machine of those parts which obstruct easy removal of the cylinder or cylinder head, as the case may be.

Removing Petrol Tank. This is necessary prior to decarbonizing all 1932-9 O.H.C. models, including the "Internationals." On the S.V. models, removal of the tank is not necessary, but in the case of the push-rod O.H.V. engines its removal will be found most advantageous. The petrol tank on all 1932 models may be taken off after disconnecting the petrol feed by removing the four fixing bolts and drawing the tank backwards and upwards. On 1933-47 models, to remove the petrol tank, place petrol taps in the "off" position and disconnect the petrol pipes. It is not necessary to drain the tank. Unscrew the four fixing bolts which attach the tank to the frame platforms, and in the case of all electrically-equipped models with tank panels, remove the seven slotted head screws which attach the panel to the tank. This will enable the panel to be lifted sufficiently to allow the tank to be easily removed. If a speedometer is fitted, disconnect the drive at the speedometer end. (See also page 110.)

Decarbonizing S.V. Models (1932-7). Unless it is desired to examine the piston on these models, it is sufficient to remove the detachable head only, and the carburettor and valves need not be disturbed. To take off the head, remove the sparking plug, undo the nine nuts holding the head to the barrel, and break the joint. Should this be difficult, give the bottom fins on the head a smart tap sideways, using a lead hammer or interposing a piece of wood between an ordinary hammer and the fins. The carbon may then be scraped off the piston crown, the combustion chamber, and valves as described on page 79 with a blunt screwdriver or knife. To remove the cylinder barrel, detach the carburettor, exhaust pipe, and exhaust valve lifter cable at the cylinder, remove valve cover, put the piston near B.D.C., with both valves closed, and after removing the four base nuts draw off while supporting the piston in the hand (see Fig. 41).

Place a rag over the crankcase hole. The piston may then be removed by pushing out the gudgeon-pin after removing one of the wire circlips with a small pair of round-nosed pliers. Remove and examine the rings and clean the piston, as described on pages 78-80.

Before reassembly and before refitting the piston, drain the crankcase of all dirty oil and swill out with flushing oil. See that

ADJUSTMENTS AND OVERHAULING

all dirt is swilled out from the base of the sump. Pour some fresh oil over the flywheels and big-end. (See page 46.)

To refit the piston place it over the small-end and push in the floating gudgeon-pin (which should be oiled), afterwards replacing the wire circlip. This must spring properly into the piston boss groove but must not be forced into place. If it does not enter easily, place one jaw of the pliers over the wire and the other over the piston boss. Now refit cylinder barrel (Fig. 42) after smearing

FIG. 41. REMOVING CYLINDER BARREL (S.V.)
The barrel must be lifted off vertically on 1937-47 O.H.V. models. Be careful not to move it sideways as this may bend the connecting rod. Also block up the crankcase hole with a rag when removing the barrel.

the piston with oil, and if the rings do not enter easily obtain assistance. Screw down the cylinder nuts in a diagonal order, giving each a half-turn after contacting with the cylinder flange. Tighten the cylinder head nuts evenly in the same way.

Do not forget to replace the copper washer between the cylinder-head and barrel. Also take great care with the paper washer which makes a joint between the top of the crankcase and the cylinder base. There must be a hole in the washer so that the oil hole in the crankcase, and the corresponding hole in the cylinder barrel, are not cut off by this washer (i.e. the washer hole must be directly over and slightly larger than the crankcase hole). Finally refit the carburettor, exhaust pipe, plug and exhaust lifter. Check over the valve clearances (page 61), warm up the engine and after cooling go over the cylinder-head and barrel nuts again.

The valves, which should not be interchanged, may be removed with a suitable valve extractor before or after taking off the cylinder-head, and should be ground-in. (See also page 113.)

Decarbonizing O.H.V. Engines (1932-7). Firstly, remove carburettor, sparking plug, and exhaust pipe(s). See that the engine is revolved to such a position that both valves are on their seats, i.e. that there is a clearance between the ball-ended rocker

Fig. 42. Refitting Cylinder Barrel (O.H.V.)

If difficulty is experienced in getting the piston rings to enter the cylinder, you should get someone to hold the cylinder. See that the ring slots are spaced at 120 degrees and avoid damaging the elongated studs on 1937 and later O.H.V. models. Oil the piston before insertion in the bore.

adjuster screws and valve stems. On 1935-7 engines disconnect the two small valve guide lubricating pipes. Unscrew the cheesehead screws which hold the rocker-box cover in position; this will enable the cover to be removed and the push-rod cover tubes can then be slackened in their top housing. Slacken the gland nuts which hold these tubes to the crankcase. The four holding-down bolts (*E*, Fig. 53), which hold the rocker-box, can now be removed and the rocker-box taken away; this will enable the four cylinder-head sleeve nuts to be unscrewed. If difficulty is experienced in detaching the cylinder-head from the barrel, a tap under the inlet port, using a lead hammer or interposing a piece of wood between an ordinary hammer and the inlet port, should loosen the head. To remove the cylinder barrel, piston, and rings,

ADJUSTMENTS AND OVERHAULING

proceed as for the S.V. engines. Remove all carbon from the piston (including the rings and underside), combustion chamber and ports as decribed on page 79. To remove the valves and grind them in, follow the advice on page 80. Note also the remarks on page 82 about grinding-in the cylinder-head and barrel faces. When reassembling the piston, cylinder-head and barrel, note the hints on page 75 and take great care with regard to the paper washer below the cylinder barrel, as mentioned previously in the hints on decarbonizing the S.V. engines. Hermatite jointing compound is recommended for the cylinder-head joint, but engine oil can be used. Reassembling is practically a reversal of the procedure for dismantling, but note that no washer is used for the cylinder-head. Refit the carburettor, rocker-box, push-rods, and exhaust pipe. Then run up the engine, allow to cool, go over the nuts again, and adjust the valve clearances. (See Appendix.)

Decarbonizing O.H.C. Models (pre-1947). Remove the tank, oil pipe from the pump to the rocker-box, carburettor, exhaust pipe, sparking plug, and remove the four rocker-box bolts and take away the distance pieces (Models CS1, CJ) between the cylinder-head bolts and rocker-box. Completely unscrew the vertical shaft cover tube top gland nut, unscrew the bottom gland nut several turns, remove the rocker-box bevel inspection cover, and turn the engine over until the piston is on T.D.C. and the marks on the camshaft bevel and vertical shaft top bevel coincide, place machine in gear to prevent the piston moving from T.D.C. position.

If the rocker-box and vertical shaft tube are now tilted slightly away from the cylinder barrel and the rocker-box is then lifted approximately $\frac{1}{2}$ in. to clear the top vertical shaft coupling, the rocker-box may be withdrawn sideways. Disconnect the cylinder-head torque stays used on the "Internationals." Unscrew the cylinder-head nuts and the joint between the cylinder-head and barrel may then be broken. If the head is difficult to separate from the barrel, a tap under the inlet port, using a lead hammer or interposing a piece of wood between the port and hammer, should loosen the head. The barrel can now be readily taken off if necessary. Valve removing, grinding-in, and refitting barrel and head are exactly the same as on the O.H.V. push-rod engines.

Removing O.H.C. Rocker-box. The simplest method is to detach the top bevel housing from the rocker-box by removing the four nuts. The mesh of the bevels is marked, but it will be necessary to see that the contact-breaker of the magneto is in the same position relative to the camshaft when reassembling as before, otherwise the sparking plug will be firing on the wrong stroke and the magneto will have to be retimed. Do not detach the vertical shaft, vertical shaft bevels or bevel housings from the vertical shaft tube.

Examining and Removing Piston Rings. The piston rings are the main-guard of the compression. They must, therefore, be full of spring, free in their grooves, and set with their slots opposite to each other (i.e. at 120° in the case of the three-ring piston which is fitted on all type Norton engines). If all three rings are bright all the way round, they are obviously being polished against the cylinder walls, and are perfect, and should be left alone. If, on the other hand, they are dull or stained at some points, they are not in proper contact with the walls of the cylinder. Perhaps they are stuck in their grooves with burnt oil, and will function properly if the grooves are cleaned. If vertically loose in their grooves or very badly marked, the rings must be renewed. Piston rings are of cast-iron and, being of very small section, must be handled very, very carefully. If not, they will certainly be broken. They cannot safely be opened out wider than will allow them to slip over the crown of the piston. Therefore, to put them on or remove them requires the insertion of small strips of metal, about ½ in. wide by 2 in. long, which are placed in the manner illustrated by Fig. 44. Be most careful to note the order in which the rings are removed so as to ensure proper replacement. When fitting new piston rings, thoroughly clean the grooves into which they fit, as any deposit left at the back of new rings forces them out and makes them too tight a fit. Paraffin usually loosens stuck piston rings. Piston rings are made to very accurate dimensions, and it is very bad practice to attempt to "fit" oversize or undersize rings unless you know exactly what you are doing. Lapping-in oversize piston rings is a skilful job, and unless the slot sizes are exactly right, the rings will not function well, and may even produce an engine "seizure." Therefore, always use piston rings supplied by Norton Motors, Ltd. The correct gap at the slots for all plain rings is ·015 in.–·020 in. and for the oil control rings ·008 in. (See also page 114.)

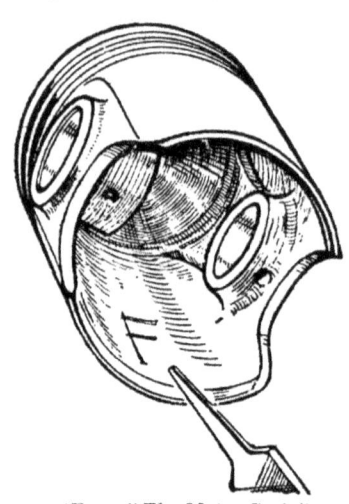

(*From "The Motor-Cycle"*)
Fig. 43. Marking Inside of Piston to Ensure Correct Replacement

ADJUSTMENTS AND OVERHAULING

Removing the Carbon. Thoroughness in decarbonizing well repays the labour expended. To clean the cylinder-head, the best tool is a blunt knife or screw-driver, with which the carbon can be scraped and chipped from the head, great care being taken to see that the combustion chamber is not deeply scratched.

Remove all traces of carbon from the interior surfaces and do not forget the sparking plug hole and the exhaust port. Carbon

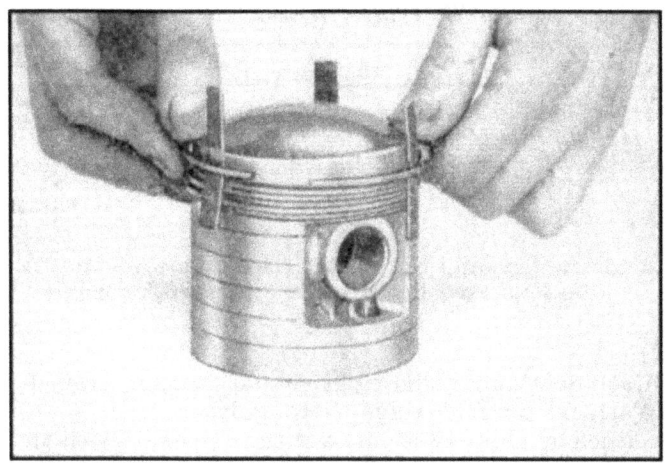

FIG. 44. A SAFE METHOD OF REMOVING AND FITTING PISTON RINGS

forms less readily on a smooth surface and therefore it is a good plan to polish the inside of the head with fine emery cloth, but do this before removing the valves, and afterwards clean all abrasive particles away with petrol. Also scrape all carbon from the valve heads.

In the case of the O.H.V. head, care should be taken that the ground joint of the head is not damaged. The method adopted at the Works of holding the head whilst decarbonizing is to fit a hexagon steel bar screwed at one end into the sparking plug hole. The cylinder head may then be held in a vice by means of the steel bar. If such a bar is not available, an old sparking plug makes a useful substitute. This will facilitate the operation considerably.

With the comparatively soft aluminium piston be most careful when removing the carbon. Do not use emery cloth, the carbon being removed by means of a blunt knife or screwdriver alone and the surface afterwards wiped with a rag damped in petrol.

Make no attempt to remove carbon from the skirt. A lot of carbon is usually deposited on the *inside* of the piston. It is most important that this should be removed. The screw-driver can be used for this till all carbon is scraped off the ribs, etc., inside piston. Take care not to let screw-driver shank bump unnecessarily against piston skirt, or the latter may crack. Examine ring grooves for carbon. Should any be present, scrape

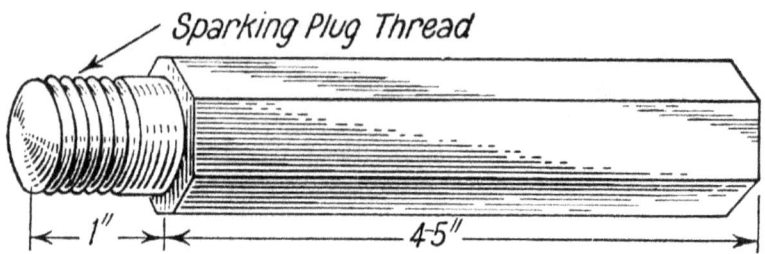

Fig. 45. A Hexagon Steel Bar Turned and Threaded at one End to Hold the Cylinder Head when Decarbonizing

out with a blunt knife. The rings should also be scraped at the back. Wash piston and rings thoroughly in clean petrol. Refit rings either by slipping them over the piston or with the three strips previously described.

Removing Valves (Side-by-Side Type). The valves may be removed whilst the cylinder is on the crankcase or after detaching the cylinder barrel, by means of a proprietary spring compressor such as the Terry illustrated in Fig. 46A. This should be placed, after removing the cylinder head, so that the hook rests on the valve head. The lever portion should be placed under valve spring cap and the lever depressed; when the spring is lifted to its full extent, fix the ratchet arm in position. Both hands are now free to remove the valve cotters. On all Norton side-valve models split type valve cotters are fitted, and these may be easily removed with the fingers. Remove valve-lifter tool; the valve can then be removed, as also can the spring.

Removal of Valves (Overhead Type). This can be accomplished by the aid of a tool, such as the Terry O.H.V. valve spring compressor shown in Fig. 46B. To remove the split valve cotters used on all O.H.V. engines as well as S.V. engines, place the spring compressor with the forked end resting on the valve spring cap or plate, in the case of the hairpin valve springs, and the end of the screw in the centre of the valve. Then tighten the screw until

ADJUSTMENTS AND OVERHAULING

the spring is compressed enough to enable the split cotters to be removed. The valve can then be drawn out.

Grinding-in the Valves. Should the valve faces or seats show signs of serious pitting, the valves will have to be ground-in. Do not grind them in whenever you decarbonize, as excessive grinding causes the valves to become "pocketed." About once

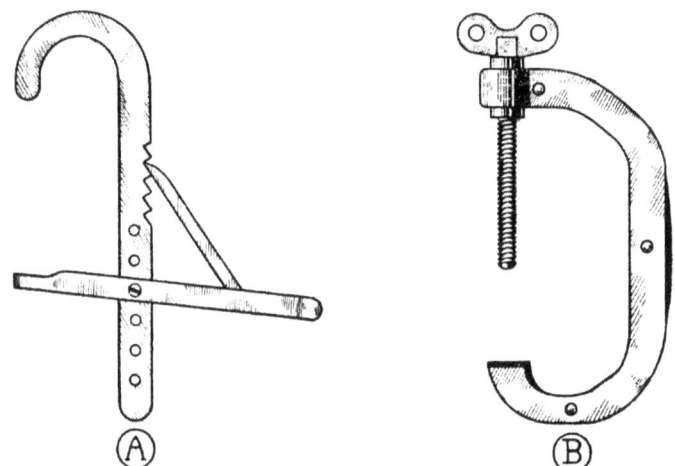

FIG. 46. TWO USEFUL VALVE SPRING COMPRESSORS

Both the above tools are obtainable from H. Terry & Sons, Ltd. That shown at A is for S.V. engines and that at B for O.H.V. and O.H.C. engines.

every 10,000 miles should be sufficient if the valve clearances are correctly maintained. Valves of the side-by-side type have, of course, to be *pressed down* on their seatings when using a screwdriver, while those of the overhead type have to be pulled up against their seatings with a hand vice. (Nortons supply a tool.)

Only grind in valves when necessary, using *fine* valve-grinding compound mixed with oil or paraffin; only a small quantity is necessary, and do not revolve the valves round and round, but give a quarter turn backwards and forwards, frequently raising the valve from its seat and dropping down in a different position. A small hand vice will be found a convenient tool for holding the valve stem on O.H.V. engines, and very great care must be taken after this operation to remove all traces of valve-grinding compound. The valve stems may be cleaned with *very fine* or worn emery cloth. Do not use coarse grinding compound for grinding valves in. A little fine paste smeared very lightly over the valve face is far better. Richford's grinding paste is very suitable.

Never continue grinding-in once a perfect line seating is obtained. The bevelled edge of the valve should become bright all round, and all pitting should have disappeared. If the pitting is very extensive and deep, send the valves to the manufacturers to be refaced. After grinding-in be exceedingly careful to remove all traces of grinding-compound and oil the valve stems before replacement. Do not interchange valves. On 1935-7 O.H.V. engines do not forget to reconnect the valve guide lubricating pipes and tighten the union nuts securely. (See also page 113.)

Grinding-in Cylinder Head and Barrel Faces. If either seatings have been damaged in removal of the head, it will be necessary to regrind these in, in the same manner as one would a valve. To grind in the cylinder head, the four studs should be removed. This may be done by screwing two nuts on the studs, using one as a lock-nut against the other. The holes from which the studs have been taken should then be filled with grease, so that the grinding compound is kept out of the threads. The head and barrels should then be rubbed together, similar to the grinding-in of valves. A good joint may be made between the head and the barrel by smearing a little Hermatite on the faces.

TUNING FOR SPEED

Considerations of space permit of this subject being barely touched upon, but a few hints are worthy of inclusion, having regard to the large number of Norton owners who use their machines in speed events.

Compression Ratio. The standard compression ratios are a trifle low for racing on special fuels, and special high compression pistons are available (O.H.V. and O.H.C.). On the camshaft engines, metal must not be removed from the cylinder base or cylinder head faces, as this interferes with the camshaft drive.

To check the compression ratio it is necessary to ascertain the cubic capacity of the combustion space; this can be done by bringing the piston to top dead-centre with valves closed (firing point) and then pouring in a very thin oil or paraffin from a graduated beaker till the space is completely filled. The beaker should be graduated in c.c.'s (cubic centimetres), and from the volume of liquid poured in, the compression ratio can be calculated, since the swept area is readily ascertainable from the bore and stroke.

The Piston. By far the greatest frictional losses in an I.C. engine occur at the piston, and when tuning for speed it is imperative to see that friction here is reduced to an absolute minimum, for when the engine is running at 4000 r.p.m., the piston covers the power stroke in approximately $\frac{1}{130}$ of a second (and the explosion will have to occur in about $\frac{1}{500}$ of a second). When a new piston has been run about 100 miles, it should be removed and very carefully examined. Presuming it is of aluminium alloy, the odds are that an inspection will reveal minute patches standing out from the slatish grey of the body by reason of the high

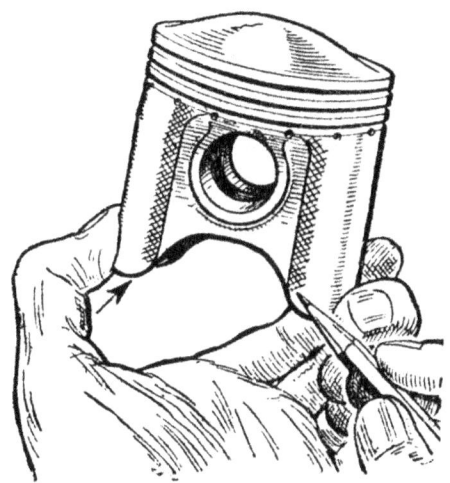

(*From "The Motor-Cycle"*)

Fig. 47. Where "High Spots" Usually Occur on a Semi-slipper Piston

polish. These patches prevent the engine from delivering its maximum speed. The rings should therefore be slipped off and the bright areas should be very, very carefully filed with a nail file. Only the minutest portion should be removed, and the duller portions should not be touched. If the piston is of the semi-slipper type, inspect the cross-shaded areas shown at Fig. 47, since here the expansion of the gudgeon pin bosses is liable to cause trouble. Do not overlook the parts indicated by the pencil. Racing men habitually remove the piston for the purpose of easing down "high spots."

Cylinder Head and Valve Ports. Time spent on polishing the head and ports is well expended, and usually productive of additional speed. The inlet port requires the chief attention, as the gas is sucked in and not displaced during the inlet stroke. The ports should be polished with riflers or bent files. Similarly, the valve stems may be burnished.

Valve Springs. For racing it is desirable to use slightly more powerful valve springs than the standard type. They can be obtained from the manufacturers.

Balancing and Lightening Moving Parts. An expert can get several extra "horses" by very carefully balancing certain parts and by taking some metal off the reciprocating members; and since only the expert can be trusted to do this, no future reference will be made to the subject.

The Carburettor. Tune for speed, and disregard fuel consumption and slow running by fitting the largest jets the engine will take. For serious track racing it is desirable to fit a racing type Amal carburettor (see page 37).

The Magneto. All parts of the magneto must be scrupulously clean, and prior to a trial or speed event, the contact-breaker should be removed, and the points cleaned and adjusted. (See page 85.) The ignition advance should be slightly greater than that used for normal running, and a racing magneto is desirable.

Gear Ratios. Very great care indeed must be taken in the selection of the top gear ratio, and experiments should be made with different-sized sprockets.

To find the top gear ratio, use the following formula—

$$\text{Top gear ratio} = \frac{\text{No. of teeth on rear sprocket}}{\text{No. of teeth on gear-box sprocket}} \times \frac{\text{No. of teeth on clutch sprocket}}{\text{No. of teeth on engine sprocket}}$$

"International" Gear Ratios. The standard gear ratios are suitable for fast road work, but for racing on any particular circuit, different gear ratios may be desirable. Various size engine sprockets are available from the manufacturers, and advice on the subject may be obtained from their Technical Department. To find the gear ratios, observe the formula above.

Pumping Losses. Avoid excessive lubrication of parts which sets up serious pumping losses, especially in the crankcase.

Exhaust Pipe Coloration. Those who do their own speed tuning, and use the coloration or discoloration of their exhaust pipes as a guide to tune, should note that chromium-plated pipes do not discolour in the usual way.

ADJUSTMENTS AND OVERHAULING

MAINTENANCE AND OVERHAULING

Care of the Lucas Type Magneto (or **Magneto Portion of " Magdyno "**). When undertaking an annual overhaul (see page 93), the following points should be attended to—

(*a*) Polish the contacts with fine emery cloth or carborundum stone and wipe clean with a petrol-damped rag. To clean the points (on the ring cam CB), it is necessary to withdraw the contact-breaker from its housing by unscrewing the hexagon-headed

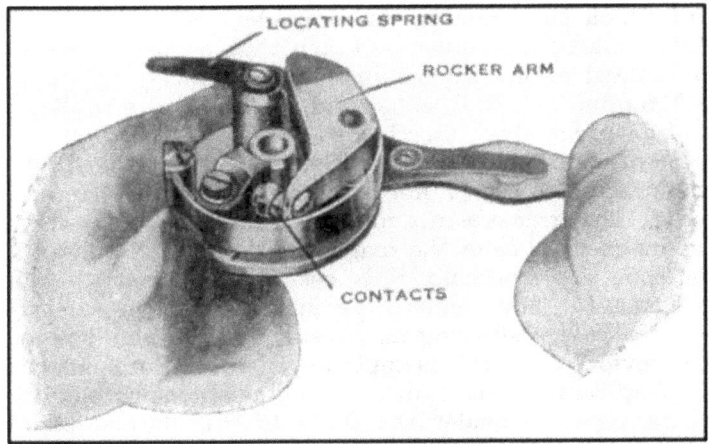

FIG. 48. REMOVAL OF LUCAS CONTACT-BREAKER ROCKER ARM FOR CLEANING CONTACTS (RING CAM TYPE)

retaining screw by means of the magneto spanner. The whole contact-breaker can then be pulled off the tapered shaft on which it fits. Now push aside the locating spring and prise the rocker-arm off its bearing, as shown in Fig. 48, when it will be possible to begin cleaning the points. Do not interfere with the spring-retaining screws. Before removing the rocker-arm, note whether the breaking of the contacts is at all sluggish by putting pressure on the fibre heel. If this is found to be the case, the bearing pin should be cleaned with very fine emery cloth and afterwards moistened with a little oil. When replacing the contact-breaker, care should be taken to ensure that the projecting key on the tapered portion of the contact-breaker base engages with the key-way cut in the armature spindle, or the whole timing of the magneto will be upset. The hexagon-headed screw should be tightened up with care; it must not be too slack (for it is part of the primary circuit), nor must undue force be used.

(*b*) If the machine has done a season's riding, get a Lucas Service depot to remove the driving end bearing plate and resoak the felt washer in good quality grease.

(c) Remove the H.T. pick-up by swinging aside the flat spring (pre-1937), and polish the moulding with a clean cloth. See that the carbon brush is working freely in its holder and that it is not unduly worn. Clean the slip-ring track and flanges by holding a soft cloth damped with petrol by means of a piece of wood on the ring while the engine is being slowly and very carefully rotated. A magneto run with a carbon brush absent, or sticking, produces nitric acid internally (due to the sparking), which destroys all the lubricant, and attacks both the metal and insulation of which the armature is composed. If the brush is accidentally broken, care must be taken that no pieces are allowed to remain inside, or serious damage will result.

(d) Examine the H.T. cable and replace if the rubber shows signs of disintegrating. (See below.)

(e) See that the contacts "break" to the correct extent (·012 in.). It is seldom necessary, nor is it desirable, to dismantle the magneto. The armature of a magneto cannot be removed without loss of magnetism from the magnet and, unless facilities for remagnetizing are available, it is best not to dismantle. If you must dismantle, first remove the pick-up and the safety spark screw, or a broken slip-ring may result. Also bridge pole pieces.

The previous instructions apply in general to Lucas instruments with a ring cam or face cam type contact-breaker, but with the face cam type, to render the contacts (Fig. 36) accessible for cleaning (or to get at the wick), remove the spring arm carrying the moving contact. If it is at all dirty, clean it thoroughly. It is important when replacing the arm to make sure that the small backing spring is fitted correctly, i.e. under the securing screw and spring washer, with the bent portion facing outwards.

Fitting High-tension Cable to Lucas Instruments. The method of re-wiring the pick-up is as follows: The cable must not be bared, but should be cut off flush to the required length. Then remove the carbon brush and spring, thus exposing to view the pointed cable securing screw. Remove this screw and push the cable hard home. Replace and tighten the screw which will secure the cable firmly, and at the same time make good contact with its core. Finally, replace the brush, spring, and pick-up.

On the later instruments, to re-wire (7 mm. cable), unscrew the terminal moulding and slip it over the lead. Burr the end of the cable for ¼ in., thread the wire through the metal washer, and bend back the strands. Then screw the moulding home.

How to Fit Bowden Cable to Lucas Spring Control (1932-3 Models). Remove the screw A (Fig. 49), then, without dismantling any part of the control, thread the Bowden cable through the cable stop *B*. Pass it through the control until it emerges at the hole left by the screw *A*. Now solder the brass nipple *C* to the end

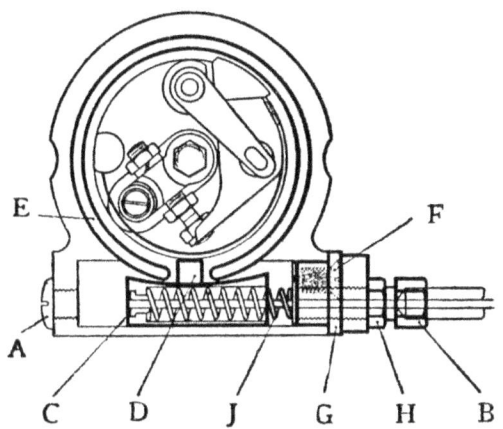

Fig. 49. Section of Lucas Spring Control (1932–3)

A = Screw
B = Cable stop
C = Brass nipple
D = Plunger
E = Cam ring
F = End-plate fixing screw
G = End plate
H = Lock-nut
J = Spring

of the cable, and then pull it from the other end until it is felt that the nipple fits into the end of the main body of the plunger *D*, when the screw *A* should be replaced. By referring to Fig. 49,

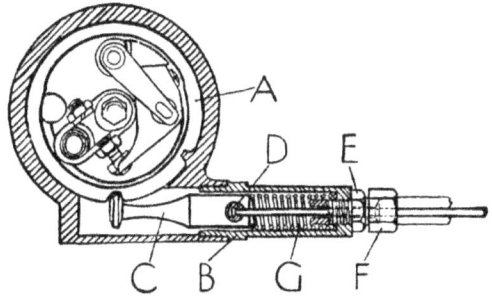

Fig. 50. Section of Lucas Spring Control (1934 onwards)

A = Ring cam
B = Cable casing
C = Plunger
D = Nipple
E = Lock-nut
F = Cable stop
G = Spring

it will be seen that on applying a tension to the Bowden cable, the plunger *D* will move the cam ring *E* and so alter the timing of the magneto.

How to Fit Bowden Cable to Lucas Spring Control (1934 Onwards). It is unnecessary to detach the ring cam. Referring to Fig. 50, remove the cable casing B by unscrewing the hexagon nut at its base. Then draw up as far as possible the cable and plunger C to which it is attached when it will be found that the nipple D on the end of the cable emerges sufficiently to be slipped sideways out of the hole in the plunger in which it fits, so completely detaching the cable. To fit the new cable thread it through the casing and solder the nipple to the end. Slip the nipple sideways into the hole in the plunger and screw the casing home. Slackness can afterwards be taken up by the cable stop F.

Removing Bowden Cable from M-L Magneto. To remove the cable from the instrument, do not attempt to remove the cam from its housing. It is only necessary to undo the hexagon nut, which forms the abutment for the outer casing of the Bowden cable. If the cable and plunger to which it is attached are drawn upwards to their fullest extent, it will be found that the nipple into which the end of the cable is soldered comes above the top of the boss on the cam cage housing. The nipple may then be slipped sideways out of the hole in the plunger in which it fits, thus detaching the cable entirely.

Ignition Timing. Exact ignition timing is extremely important. Many riders imagine that by advancing their timing they necessarily will get more speed. This is a fallacy, and it only throws unfair loads on the engine, spoiling its flexibility and, eventually, damaging it throughout. For all normal road uses, the spark settings given subsequently (see pages 89 and 104) should be closely adhered to. Only for genuine racing purposes is it advisable to increase the spark advance beyond these limits, and even then undue spark advance should be avoided. It should always be remembered that should the timing be so far advanced that maximum explosion pressures are reached with the crank in true T.D.C. position, the big-ends come in for a terrific hammering for which they are not designed. If a "Magdyno" has been removed for any purpose or the drive disturbed, it will be necessary to re-time it, and to do this proceed as follows.

Set the piston so that it is at the top of the compression stroke and as near the T.D.C. position as possible. Verify that it is on the compression and not the exhaust stroke by noting whether both valves are fully closed with the normal clearances at the tappets or rockers, as the case may be. Now remove the magneto chain case and loosen the sprocket fixed on the tapered end of the magneto armature. Probably the sprocket is rather stiff, in which case a lever may be wedged tightly at the back of the

ADJUSTMENTS AND OVERHAULING

sprocket after undoing the nut a couple of turns. Now direct a sharp tap on the sprocket nut which should free the sprocket from its taper. If it does not, employ a sprocket extractor. Keep the magneto chain on, and, if it has perchance been removed, refit it. Then remove the sparking plug or dummy plug provided for the purpose on S.V. engines, and insert a pencil or piece of wire through the hole. Make a mark on the pencil or wire, and measure carefully, and place another mark $\frac{4}{16}$ in. (or whatever the exact ignition advance is) above the first one. Rotate engine slowly backwards until the top mark occupies the place previously held by the bottom mark, the piston having obviously descended $\frac{4}{16}$ in. (or $\frac{1}{4}$ in.), as the case may be; then set the contact-breaker so that the points just commence to separate with the spark lever on *full advance*.

To find the exact point of break, place a cigarette paper between the closed points and turn the armature forwards until the paper is just released, and no more, on pulling it gently. When first tightening the spindle nut, the magneto should be held from rotating by means of the contact-breaker until the taper in the sprocket bites on the spindle. Do not, however, hold by the contact-breaker for final tightening, or the contact-breaker may be damaged.

Having checked the timing, check the gap at the contacts; replace contact-breaker cover; and then, after tensioning the magneto chain, replace the chain case cover, when the engine may be started up and tested. The magneto chain should not be tensioned by means of the magneto-retaining screws to an extent such that a bending moment is imposed on the armature spindle. It should be perceptibly slack in all positions.

Ignition Advance (1934-7 Models). On Model 16H the contacts should commence to break with the piston $\frac{7}{32}$ in. (25 degrees), before T.D.C. on full advance. On the "Big Four" the correct timing is $\frac{1}{4}$ in. (25 degrees) before T.D.C. on full advance. The timing on Models 18, 20, ES2 is $\frac{3}{4}$ in. (42 degrees) before T.D.C. on full advance for touring and $\frac{25}{32}$ in. (47 degrees) for racing. On Model 19 the timing is $\frac{5}{8}$ in. (42 degrees) before T.D.C. for touring and $\frac{7}{8}$ in. (47 degrees) for racing. The setting for Models CSI, CJ is $\frac{11}{16}$ in. (45 degrees) before T.D.C. on full advance. With regard to the Models 50, 55 the correct spark advance is $\frac{11}{16}$ in.–$\frac{3}{4}$ in. (48–50 degrees) before T.D.C. on full advance, and for Models 30, 40 it is 50–52 degrees before T.D.C. on full advance.

To check or retime the magneto or "Magdyno" proceed as described above, inserting the wire or pencil through the sparking-plug hole or, on the S.V. engines, where compression cocks are no longer provided, through the hole occupied by the dummy plug immediately above the piston centre. Note that the B.T.-H. and M.L. magnetos are in the fully-advanced position when the inner wire is slack. More exact ignition timing can, of course, be made by measuring the advance in degrees of crankshaft rotation. For this purpose a timing disc made of sheet tin or cardboard is required (Fig. 51) for attachment to the engine

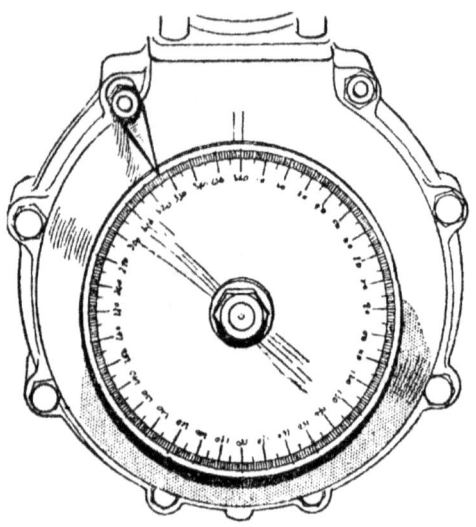

(*From "The Motor-Cycle"*)

FIG. 51. SHOWING CRANKSHAFT DEGREE DISC FOR VALVE AND IGNITION TIMING

A suitable pointer can be fixed as shown to one of the crankcase bolts. T.D.C. position must first be accurately found.

shaft. A cardboard disc can incidentally be obtained from the manufacturers of Castrol oil. It is quite easy to make a suitable disc if necessary. See page 104 for 1938–47 timings.

Ignition Advance (1932-3 Models). The settings given in the preceding paragraph are suitable with a few exceptions. On the "Big Four" give advance of $\frac{1}{4}$ in. (20 degrees) before T.D.C. On Models 18, 20 ES2 give advance of $\frac{5}{8}$ in. (42 degrees) before T.D.C. for touring and $1\frac{3}{16}$ in. (50 degrees) for racing. In the case of Model 19 give ignition advance of $\frac{3}{4}$ in. (42 degrees) before T.D.C. for touring and $1\frac{3}{16}$ in. (50 degrees) for racing.

Engine Timing (1932-7 16H, I, 18, 19, 20, ES2). The valve timing diagram shown in Fig. 52, is applicable to the whole of the S.V. and O.H.V. Norton range, except Models 50, 55, when timing is measured on the degree system, which is strongly

ADJUSTMENTS AND OVERHAULING

advocated. When timing by means of measurements taken on the piston stroke, there are certain variations which should be

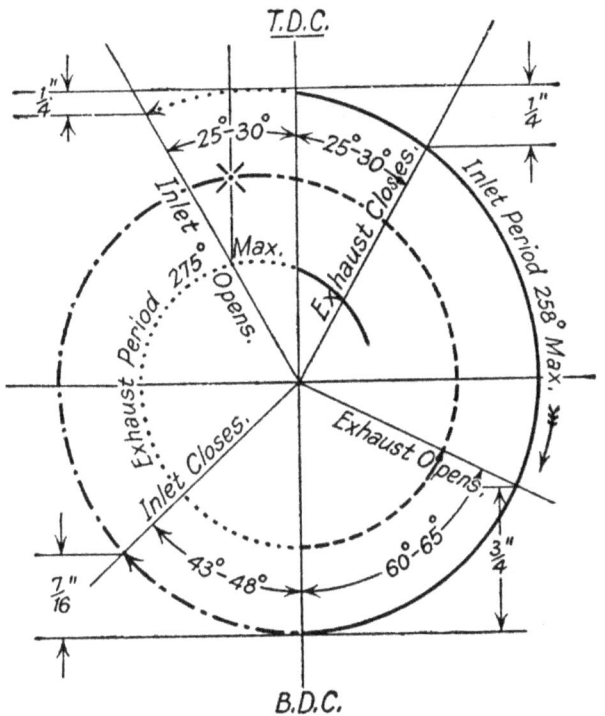

Fig. 52. Valve-timing Diagram for 1932–9 S.V. and O.H.V. Engines

The valve-timing diagram shown is applicable to all Norton S.V. and O.H.V. engines except Models 50, 55, if timing be measured by degrees of crank rotation, which is recommended. Norton Motors, Ltd., do not punch-mark their timing pinions except in the case of the "camshaft" models; and should the timing gear be dismantled, it is advisable to mark them first or else to retime. The valve clearances must be correct when retiming. When timing is effected by measuring the distance between the piston crown and the dead centres, it should be noted that on the 5·96 h.p. and 6·33 h.p. long-stroke engines lessened connecting-rod angularity necessitates the exhaust valve opening being $\frac{1}{16}$ in. earlier and the other periods being increased to the extent of $\frac{1}{16}$ in.

carefully noted. These variations are made clear in the caption below the illustration (see Fig. 52). Compression cocks are not provided on the S.V. engines, and the wire or pencil used for finding the piston advance before T.D.C. may be inserted through the hole occupied by a dummy plug immediately over the centre of the piston. Three keyways are provided on all engine pinions and if the timing is disturbed the keyway into which the key fits should be marked as well as the pinions. In the case of Models 50, 55 the inlet valve should open $\frac{5}{16}$ in.-$\frac{3}{8}$ in. (30-35 degrees) before T.D.C., and the exhaust valve should close $\frac{3}{8}$ in.-$\frac{7}{16}$ in. (35-40 degrees) after T.D.C.

Timing the engine valve gear is in many respects analogous to timing the magneto, that is to say, the piston is set at T.D.C., and the necessary advance and retard given to the inlet and exhaust valve opening and closing respectively. As a rule, the rider rarely has occasion to re-time, since the timing pinions are generally marked before dismantling, and are replaced in the same relative positions as they are extracted. Clearly the opening of the inlet valve and the closing of the exhaust valve are the only factors that have to be taken into account, for clearly the cam contours determine automatically the remaining valve action. There is, however, one very important point, and this is to ensure that the valve clearances are correct first. Without doing this, accurate timing is quite impossible.

As a rough check on the timing, "rock" the engine sprocket to and fro, so that the piston comes to the top of its stroke and slightly down, when one valve should close and the other open. Some Norton engines have detachable cams, and it is imperative to see that they are screwed firmly to the cam wheels prior to reassembly. Always time the inlet valve first and the exhaust valve afterwards, and on no account remove the engine pinion, unless essential. Time on the *exhaust* stroke (see also pages 104-105).

Engine Timing (1932-7 O.H.C. Models). On all 1932-7 O.H.C. models the valve timing should be correct if the marks on the respective bevels coincide and the peg in the camshaft bevel is opposite the groove on the end of the camshaft and the scratched line on the bevel. Oldham-type couplings are used for the vertical shaft on all O.H.C. engines, and it is thus a very simple matter to disconnect the vertical shaft and subsequently refit it in the correct position. The bevels on the main shaft and camshaft have an identical number of teeth, which means that the vertical shaft connection can only be replaced in two positions, and if care is taken to see that the piston is on T.D.C. and the contact-breaker is in the position it was in prior to disconnecting the vertical shaft joint, it is impossible for the timing to be disturbed. Except on the 1932-7 "Internationals" the valves are correctly timed when the inlet valve commences to open $\frac{3}{8}$ in. (35 degrees) before T.D.C. and the exhaust valve closes $\frac{1}{2}$ in. (40 degrees) after T.D.C. On the "International" models the

ADJUSTMENTS AND OVERHAULING

inlet valve should open 45-50 degrees before T.D.C. and the exhaust valve should close 40-45 degrees after T.D.C. When fitting new cams always check the timing, as the keyways in the cams may not be in exactly the same position as in the old cams relative to the cam contour. For 1938-47 timings, see page 104.

A Complete Overhaul. This overhaul should be treated seriously, and the whole machine should be dismantled completely. Every component should be cleaned, scrutinized, and, if necessary, replaced. The engine and gear-box must, of course, be removed from the frame for this operation. Special points to be noted in the complete overhaul are set out herewith—

FRAME. Alinement, existence of flaws or cracks, play in spring forks, looseness of steering head, wear caused by friction of all attached parts, condition of enamel.

WHEELS. Condition of roller bearings; truth of wheels, alinement, loose spokes, condition of rims, wear of tyres.

CHAINS. Excessive wear, cracked or broken rollers, joints.

ENGINE. Oil leaks, compression leaks, main bearings, valves, valve guides and tappets, overhead valve rockers, valve springs, valve seats and faces, cotters, condition of cylinder bore, piston, piston rings, play in big-end and small-end bearings, timing wheels, shafts and bearings, cams, oil pump.

GEARS. Condition of teeth on sprockets and pinions, damaged ball races and loose parts generally.

The examination should also include all control rods and cables, oil filters, clutch and brake linings, etc. To sum up, everything should be dismantled and readjusted.

Dismantling of O.H.V. Rocker-box (1932-7 Models 18, 19, 20, ES2, 50, 55). Once the rocker-box has been detached from the head, it is easy to dismantle it and to remove the rockers. Take off the rocker-box cover by undoing the six cheese-headed screws, and unscrew the rocker shaft nuts at the opposite side of the box and also the exhaust valve-lifter bolt. The top rockers, F and F_1 (Fig. 53) may then be withdrawn from their plain bearings complete with rocker shafts and the valve rockers G and G_1, which are keyed to the shafts. The rockers are adjustable for end play by means of the nuts on the driving side, and all play in excess of ·003 in. should be taken up. If much play between the bushes and rockers is discernible, the bushes should be pressed out and new ones fitted; but owing to the complete enclosure of the rockers and the fact that they are adequately lubricated, serious wear will not occur until a big mileage has been done. When reassembling do not forget the small semi-circular keys retaining the valve rockers in position on the upper rockers. These can be seen in Fig. 53.

94 THE BOOK OF THE NORTON

To Dismantle O.H.C. Rocker-box (Models CSI, CJ, 30, 40). Remove the two rocker pivot bolts and the cheese-head screws. The cover is then held only by the dowels and camshaft roller race.

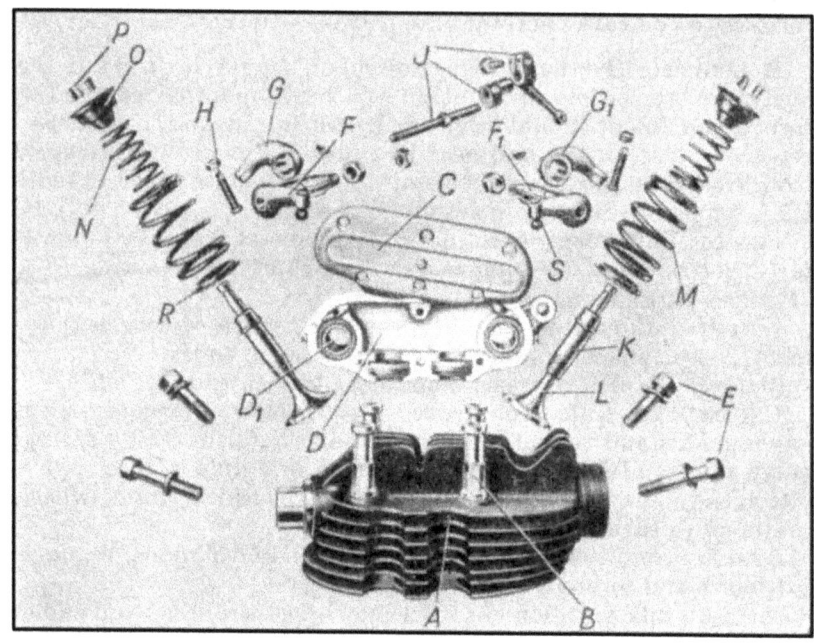

FIG. 53. SHOWING SINGLE-PORT CYLINDER HEAD WITH ROCKER-BOX AND VALVES DISMANTLED

The exploded view shown above applies to all 1932-7 O.H.V. engines, but on 1937 models valve guide lubricating pipes are included.

A = Cylinder head
B = Cylinder head sleeve nuts
C = Rocker box panel cover
D = Rocker box
D_1 = Detachable rocker bush
E = Rocker box retaining bolts
F = Top rocker and shaft (inlet)
F_1 = Top rocker and shaft (exhaust)
G = Valve rocker (inlet)
G_1 = Valve rocker (exhaust)
H = Valve rocker adjusting screw and lock-nut
J = Exhaust valve lifter mechanism
K = Valve guide
L = Tulip valve (exhaust)
M = Outer valve spring (exhaust)
N = Inner valve spring (inlet)
O = Valve spring collar (top)
P = Split collet
R = Valve spring collar (bottom)
S = Top rocker ball end

Withdraw the cover ½ in., when it will be free and can be completely removed. The rockers can now be withdrawn. These rockers are identical and it is important that they are not interchanged. A hardened insert is fixed into the end of the rocker which bears against the cams; if this has worn unduly, a new

ADJUSTMENTS AND OVERHAULING 95

insert should be fitted. To remove the cam, unscrew the L.H. threaded nut and pull off the roller race cam. The vertical shaft housings can be removed after unscrewing the four holding-down nuts at each end and raising the rocker-box so that the housings are clear of the locating spigots.

When Refitting O.H.C. Rockers. Care must be taken with the packings, otherwise trouble will be experienced from oil leakage. At the ends of the rocker bosses a resilient cork washer is fitted, but a steel washer is interposed between the end of the rocker and the cork washer in order to prevent the rocker working on the cork itself. If this washer has worn it must be replaced. Felt pads are used to seal the joint on the top and bottom of the rocker boss; these must be adjusted so that they press on to this boss moderately tight, but not so tight that the rockers bind.

Removing Timing Cover (All Models). Take off "Magdyno" chain case, remove the chain, and after loosening the spindle nuts a few turns, draw off the sprockets with an extractor, or by wedging a tyre lever between each sprocket and the case, and giving a sharp tap on the nut. Now remove the cheese-head timing cover screws, and also the two countersunk head screws inside the "Magdyno" chain case. The timing cover may then be withdrawn. The pump-drive worm on S.V. and O.H.V. models prevents the exhaust camwheel coming adrift while doing this. (See page 105.)

Examine Restriction Jet (O.H.C.s). Whenever the timing cover is removed the restriction jet, which is fitted to it and abuts the drilled main shaft through which oil passes to the big-end, should be examined to make sure that the jet is unobstructed (see notes on page 106). It is advisable also to syringe out all oil holes.

To Remove Oil Pump. In the case of all O.H.C. models, after removing the timing cover, unscrew the two screw-driver headed bolts and insert in their place two $\frac{1}{4}$ in. diameter rods, letting same protrude from the oil pump body a few inches, so that they may be gripped and the whole pump body revolved, which will free same and enable the complete unit to be withdrawn. On the Norton S.V. and O.H.V. models it is only necessary to remove the two nuts which secure the pump in position on its machined face. On reassembly, use a jointing compound such as Hermatite.

Don't Dismantle Oil Pump Unless Essential. To take apart the oil pump fitted to the S.V. and O.H.V. models, remove the four cheese-head screws from the upper cover when the covers may be taken off, exposing the gears (Fig. 26). Before removing these, scratch or mark each gear to ensure correct replacement. The fitting of new parts is best undertaken by the manufacturers. End-play in the gears (i.e. between the end-face of the gears and the cover plate) must not exceed ·002 in., and must not be too small or force will be required to rotate the driving worm, and this will lead to wear on the worm and worm wheel.

Method of Exposing Twist-grip (Internal Type) Throttle Cable. Disconnect the front-brake lever control cable from the anchor-plate lever, remove set-screw below the handlebar lever, and withdraw the latter. The cable may then be detached from the lever. Now pull off the twist-grip while rotating it anti-clockwise and the end of the cable will be exposed.

To Dismantle 1932-3 Multi-spring S.A. Clutches. Unscrew the nuts on the outside of the clutch spring-box plate and afterwards withdraw the springs and spring boxes. The spring-box plate and the other clutch plates may then be withdrawn. Note carefully their relative positions to ensure proper replacement. If it is necessary to clean the plates, use petrol, not paraffin.

Shock-absorber Screws are Burred Over. For this reason dismantling the shock absorber may be somewhat difficult, and unless the rubbers are much worn, this portion of the clutch should be left alone. The driver can be detached after removing the four screws, and the rubbers taken out of the slots in the body of the clutch sprocket. Carefully note the positions of the rubbers. Those on the driving side are solid, while those on the opposite side have small holes in them. The above applies to earlier models with shock-absorbers incorporated in the clutch sprocket.

To Remove the Clutch Sprocket (S.A. Shock-absorber). Unscrew the six nuts on the clutch spring studs, when the small plate and sprocket can be removed. The bearing is composed of alternate 1¼ in. diameter balls and rollers. These should be assembled with grease.

To Remove Oil Bath (1934-39). Dismantling the clutch on the 1934 and later models necessitates detaching the chain case cover. To do this, disconnect the brake pedal and also the exhaust pipe (if one is fitted on the near side). Then remove the footrest and take off the large nut screwed on the footrest tube. Removal of this nut enables the cover to be withdrawn exposing the primary chain and clutch (Fig. 54). When doing this be careful to ease off the cover equally all round and not to damage in any way the

ADJUSTMENTS AND OVERHAULING

oil sealing rubber band. When replacing the cover it is important to avoid using excessive force while tightening the footrest tube nut. This should only be done up tight enough to hold the cover firmly and evenly in contact with the rubber band. (See page 127.)

To Dismantle Clutch (1934 Onwards). Remove the clutch spring screws and take out the springs and spring boxes. Next remove the spring circlip surmounting the clutch body by inserting a

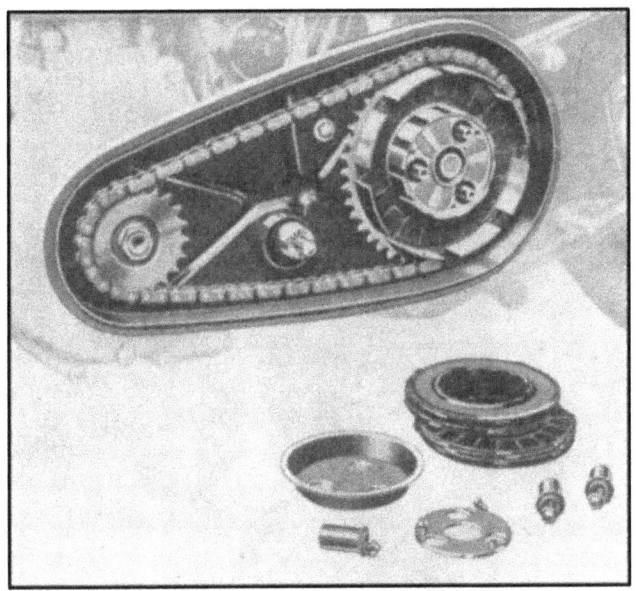

FIG. 54. SHOWING OIL BATH CHAIN CASE WITH COVER REMOVED AND CLUTCH DISMANTLED
Note the vane type rubber shock-absorber incorporated in the clutch body.

screwdriver beneath the spring and lifting it from its retaining groove. The plates can now be withdrawn and note the order in which they are fitted to ensure correct replacements. (See page 128.)

How to Dismantle Vane Type Shock-absorber. To dismantle the vane type clutch shock-absorber (Fig. 54) fitted for 1934 onwards, unscrew the three countersunk head screws holding the retaining plate on the outside of the clutch body. It is then possible to withdraw the rubbers unless they have been in use a long time and have become stuck, in which case a penknife should be used to free them from the metal vanes.

To Dismantle Three-speed Gearbox. Disconnect the clutch control wire, then remove seven cover nuts and gently pull off the cover plate. Do not use a screwdriver or similar tool to part the joint or the latter will fail to retain oil when reassembled. If the plate sticks, one or two light blows inside the kick-starter crank will loosen it. This will expose the complete interior to view. By disconnecting gear control rod the low and middle gear pinions, also layshaft, may be lifted out. When replacing, take

Fig. 55. 1939 Norton Four-speed Gearbox with Cover Removed

care that the ball bearings are not tilted. No forcing is necessary when replacing the cover plate.

Dismantling and Assembling 1933-9 Four-speed Gearbox. To dismantle completely it is necessary to remove the gearbox. Disconnect the primary chain and clutch wire, and before slackening the pivot mounting pins and adjuster, disconnect the gear control.

To facilitate dismantling the gearbox, it is best held on a ½ in. diameter bar clamped vertically in a vice. The cover end of the box should be uppermost. Having removed the kick-starter

ADJUSTMENTS AND OVERHAULING

crank and levered off the return spring cover, the return spring may be removed. The clutch operating mechanism should now be removed from the gearbox cover. The removal of the grease nipple ended pin from the end of the positive footchange shaft releases the neutral indicator and enables the operating lever to be withdrawn. Remove the aluminium cover from the positive mechanism, the lever from behind the housing, and unscrew the two nuts which hold the mechanism into position. The whole of this mechanism may now be withdrawn, with the exception of the two securing studs and the cam plate which should not require removal.

Before removing the end cover, it is advisable to place a tubular distance piece of suitable dimensions on the clutch end of the mainshaft, holding this into position with the clutch nut. This will effectively stop the shaft from being withdrawn with the cover, should it be a little tight in the cover bearing. The end cover should now be removed, which will enable the kick-starter axle to be withdrawn from its bush. The removal of the pawl pin from the enlarged end of the kick-starter axle will enable the pawl, plunger, and spring to be removed. The first pair of gears may be withdrawn from the mainshaft and layshaft, also the mainshaft second gear, together with its bush which is a running fit on the shaft and wheel. Unscrew the striking fork shaft when the layshaft second gear and striking fork may be withdrawn, followed by the mainshaft third gear and the striking fork. The layshaft may now be removed, bringing with it the remaining gears, and afterwards the mainshaft should be withdrawn. It should be noted that the removal of the mainshaft leaves the rollers on which the sleeve gear runs free to drop out, and care should be taken that none of these is lost. The gearbox should now be inverted on the bar to enable the sleeve gear to be more readily removed. The withdrawal of the axle sprocket will enable the sleeve gear to be tapped through its journal bearings in the box. Having removed the plug which carries the cam plate locating plunger, the cam plate and quadrant may be removed. This leaves the gearbox and cover with only the journal bearings and kick-starter bush, the removal of which if ever necessary should be simple.

Dismantling 1946-7 Four-speed Gearbox. This gearbox is substantially the same as the 1939 four-speed gearbox. The internal mechanism and the gear ratios are identical. The outer cover, however, now conceals the whole of the clutch and positive footchange mechanism, clutch adjustment (see page 117) being effected through an aperture fitted with a neat clip-in cover. Instructions for dismantling the 1946-7 four-speed gearbox are given in the Appendix, page 120.

APPENDIX

Throttle Stop on 1946-7 Models. On the post-war Nortons (S.V. and O.H.V.) a new type of throttle stop (see Fig. 56) is provided to render it possible to shut the throttle twist-grip right off without actually stopping the engine. To make an adjustment, first obtain good slow running in accordance with the procedure outlined on page 33.

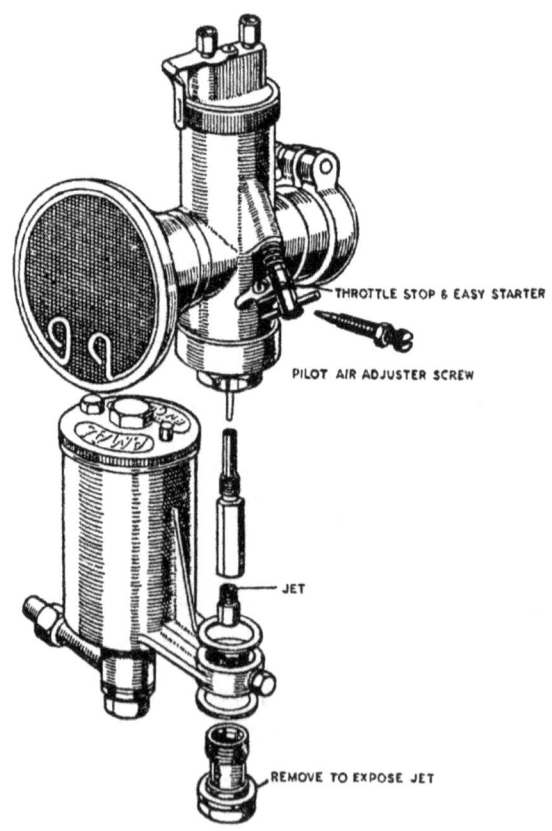

Fig. 56. Partly Exploded View of Post-war Amal Carburettor, showing Throttle Stop and Easy Starter

Now with a screwdriver, slacken the small locking pin. Then, while holding the shaped stop-piece with the left thumb in

APPENDIX

contact with the body of the mixing chamber, turn the adjuster until the engine r.p.m. are heard to increase slightly. Turn the adjuster back until the engine r.p.m. return to normal tick-over speed, and finally retighten the screw.

To ensure quick starting up, turn the adjuster as far as possible *clockwise*, so as to raise the throttle slide to the best starting position. As soon as the engine has started, return the adjuster to its normal position.

Carburettor Settings on Post-war Nortons.

The accompanying table shows the correct carburettor settings for 1946-7 side-valve and overhead-valve models. Instructions for tuning the carburettor will be found on page 33. To remove the needle jet from the drum-shaped throttle slide, remove the spring clip at the top

CARBURETTOR SETTINGS FOR S.V. AND O.H.V. MODELS (1946 Onwards)

Model (Norton)	Carb. Type Number	Main Jet Size	Throttle Valve	Needle Position
16H	276 AT	170	6/4	Middle
1	276 AT	160	6/5	Middle
18	276 AU	160	6/4	Middle
ES2	276 AU	160	6/4	Middle

of the slide. Normally the needle is fitted into the middle notch. The lower the position of the needle, the weaker is the mixture. When entering the needle into the needle jet on assembling the carburettor, be most careful not to use any force. A bent needle gives endless trouble.

Concerning Engine Lubrication (1946-7 S.V., O.H.V.).

The lubrication system on the post-war models is almost identical to that used on the 1939 Nortons and calls for little additional comment. The instructions given in Chapter IV have been checked over carefully, and will be found fully comprehensive and up to date.

Oil flows from the tank to the twin gear type oil pump, helped by suction from the feed side of the pump, through the gears, and is pressure-fed to various parts of the engine, including the rear wall of the cylinder, the big-end and the pressure control valve. Oil drains from the cylinder down the sides of the crankcase, and is conveyed via ducts to the main bearings and timing gear bearings. The valve gear, "Magdyno" chain and secondary chain are lubricated by oil mist. After circulating, the oil drains to the sludge trap and is forced back to the oil tank by the return side of the pump, which has double the capacity of the delivery side.

The oil pressure control valve is a spring-loaded ball, and functions similarly to a safety valve. It is fitted in a boss on the inside of the timing panel. When oil pressure raises the valve off its seat, oil passes the valve and is sprayed on the timing gears. It is inadvisable to remove the ball from the valve unless there is reason to think that the ball is failing to seat, or is sticking. At the Norton Works the ball spring adjusting screw is screwed right home and then released $1\frac{1}{2}$ threads. Do not tamper with this adjustment unnecessarily. Incidentally, there is no other adjustment provided in the lubrication system. If for any reason the oil control valve is dismantled, the correct order of assembly is: the ball itself; the spring; the adjuster nut. Tighten the latter fully and then screw it out $1\frac{1}{2}$ turns. Afterwards lock it with a centre punch.

Do not replenish the oil tank (see page 21) above the three-quarter full mark, otherwise building up of pressure will force surplus oil on to the road via the tank air release pipe. The effect of running with the oil below the half-full mark is to reduce the volume of oil in circulation to an extent which may cause overheating. Always remember to drain the oil tank and clean the filter every 2000 miles, and to drain the crankcase when decarbonizing. Top up the tank as required.

Replenishing Telescopic Type Front Forks. "Roadholder" telescopic type front forks with hydraulic damping are fitted as standard to all 1947 Norton models. These forks, first tried out in road racing, require to be replenished with damping oil about every 5000 miles. Suitable damping oils for the purpose are: Wakefield's Castrolite, Single Shell, or Price's Motorine E.

To replenish the forks, remove the hexagon-headed filler plug from the top of each fork leg. Then remove the drain plug from each fork end and allow all damping oil to drain out. Complete draining is assisted by operating the forks a few times manually. Replace the two drain plugs and replenish each fork leg with a measured *quarter pint* of one of the above-mentioned damping oils. Afterwards operate the forks several times to eliminate air locks, and finally replace the two filler plugs.

Adjusting Valve Clearances (1946-7 S.V., O.H.V.). The correct valve clearances for Norton engines are tabulated on page 61, and the post-war Nortons have a similar type of adjustment for both S.V. and O.H.V. engines. The adjustment is illustrated in Fig. 57 and Fig. 34 repectively. All adjustments must be made with the engine *cold*, and it is important first to verify that the exhaust valve lifter is quite clear of the exhaust valve when the piston is at T.D.C. on the compression stroke. On O.H.V. engines a clearance of *nil* implies that the push-rods must be just free to rotate without any up-and-down movement.

To make a valve clearance adjustment on a post-war S.V. or O.H.V. Norton engine, loosen the middle hexagon (lock-nut) by

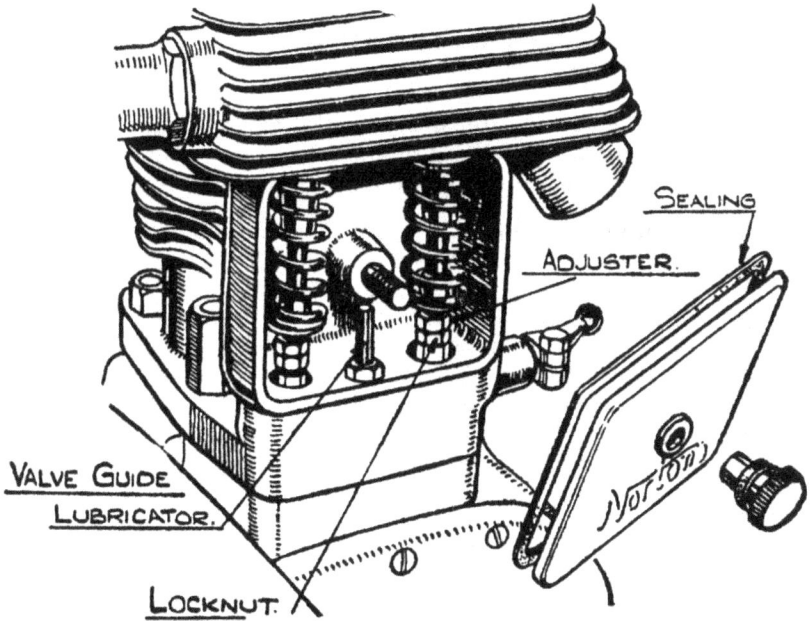

FIG. 57. TAPPET ADJUSTMENT ON POST-WAR S.V. NORTON ENGINES

The adjustment on the O.H.V. engines is identical except that it is at the top of the push-rods.

holding with one spanner the bottom hexagon on the tappet stem or push-rod, and applying a spanner to the middle hexagon. Then turn the top hexagon of the tappet head or push-rod adjuster as required to obtain the correct valve clearance. Tighten the middle hexagon and again check the clearance. Deal with both tappets or push-rods similarly.

Where Engine Number has Suffix " Q." Special care must be taken when adjusting the valve clearances of all S.V. and O.H.V. engines which have the engine number followed by the letter

"Q." The reason for this is that such engines have a modified cam-form requiring a different procedure, which is as follows:

To adjust the clearance for the inlet valve, turn the engine until the exhaust valve is just lifting. Then adjust the tappet or push-rod as described above. Similarly, to adjust the exhaust valve clearance, turn the engine until the inlet valve has just closed, and proceed to make the required adjustment. The correct valve clearance for S.V. engines is ·010 in. for both valves. On O.H.V. engines both push-rods should be just free to rotate without vertical movement.

When Removing the Timing Cover (S.V., O.H.V.). It is advisable when occasion is had to remove the timing cover to remove also the bush which carries the bronze jet feeding the big-end. The hole into which the bush is screwed (L.H. thread) must be thoroughly cleaned. All holes should also be syringed out with petrol to remove any foreign particles.

1938-9 Ignition Timings. The ignition timings given on page 89 are applicable to the 1938-9 Nortons except for the following. With the push-rod O.H.V. engine of Model 19, the platinum points of the contact-breaker should be just commencing to break when the piston is $\frac{23}{32}$ in. (or 42 degrees) before T.D.C. This is for touring only. The timing for racing is as hitherto. The correct ignition timing (measured in degrees of crankshaft rotation) for the two overhead-camshaft "International" Models 30, 40, is $42\frac{1}{2}$ degrees before T.D.C., with ignition lever fully *advanced*.

1946-7 Ignition Timings. The correct ignition timings for Models 16H and the "Big Four" are $\frac{7}{16}$ in. and $\frac{3}{8}$ in. before T.D.C. respectively, with the ignition lever fully *advanced*. For Models 18 and ES2, the correct timing is $\frac{5}{8}$ in. before T.D.C., also with the ignition lever fully *advanced*.

1938-9 Valve Timings. On S.V. and O.H.V. push-rod engines the valve timings are the same as for 1937 and the instructions on page 90 apply. On the four O.H.C. engines the method of timing given on page 92 should be followed, but the correct timings are as follows.

On Models CSI, CJ the inlet valve should commence to open $32\frac{1}{2}$ degrees ($\frac{3}{8}$ in., CSI; $\frac{11}{32}$ in., CJ) before T.D.C. and close $57\frac{1}{2}$ degrees ($1\frac{3}{32}$ in., CSI; $\frac{15}{16}$ in., CJ) after B.D.C. The exhaust valve should begin to open 70 degrees ($1\frac{1}{16}$ in., CSI; $\frac{15}{16}$ in., CJ) before B.D.C. and close 30 degrees ($\frac{5}{16}$ in., CSI; $\frac{9}{32}$ in., CJ) after T.D.C. It should be particularly noted that the above timings should be obtained with ·005 in. clearance at both valves, not with the normal running clearances. The correct timing for the

"International" models (30, 40) is such that the inlet valve opens 47½ degrees before T.D.C. and closes 70 degrees after B.D.C. The exhaust valve should open 85 degrees before B.D.C. and close 60 degrees after T.D.C.

1946-7 Valve Timings. On all 1946-7 side-valve and overhead-valve models the inlet valve opens the same distance before T.D.C. as the exhaust valve closes after T.D.C. For Model 16H it is $\frac{9}{32}$ in.; for the "Big Four," $\frac{3}{8}$ in.; for Models 18 and ES2, $\frac{5}{16}$ in. The general advice given on page 92 applies and retiming is simple, as the timing gears are normally marked for correct meshing. Exact timing is essential, and the valve clearances must be correct when checking it. When retiming engines which

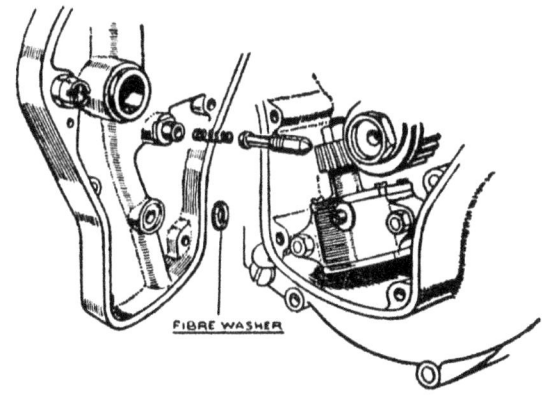

FIG. 58. REMOVAL OF TIMING COVER AND RESTRICTION JET

have the engine number followed by the suffix "Q," a ·017 in. feeler gauge should be inserted between each cam and crankcase rocker pad. Adjust the valve clearance afterwards with feeler gauge in position.

Detailed instructions for assembling the timing gears and oil pump are given on pages 106–108. These apply to all S.V. and O.H.V. post-war models.

Removing S.V., O.H.V. Timing Cover (1946 to 1947). First unscrew the three cheese-headed screws and remove the "Magdyno" chain-case cover. Remove both sprockets with the chain in position. They are a taper fit, and the camwheel sprocket is also keyed. If difficulty in removal is experienced, use a suitable withdrawal tool. Then remove the timing cover, which is secured by seven cheese-headed screws and two counter-sunk screws, the latter being in the "Magdyno" chain case. Having removed all nine screws, partly withdraw the timing cover so as to expose the timing gears and rockers. To prevent the inlet camwheel and the rockers coming adrift, hold them in place with a screwdriver while completely withdrawing the timing cover. When the timing cover is removed, the restriction jet for the big-end will leave its holder because of the spring pressure behind it. Finally, remove the spring (see Fig. 58) from its holder.

Replacing Timing Cover (1946 to 1947). To replace the timing cover on the S.V. and O.H.V. engines, first clean the edges of the timing cover and timing chest. Next smear the mating surfaces with some jointing compound or gold-size, and check the fibre washer (see Fig. 58) between the oil pump and the timing cover. Offer up the timing cover and verify that when in position the fibre washer prevents the edge of the cover contacting the timing chest by $\frac{1}{32}$ in. This spacing is necessary to ensure an oil-tight joint when the timing cover is screwed home and the washer is compressed. Finally, fit the spring and the restriction jet in its holder, and evenly and firmly tighten all nine timing cover securing screws.

Removing and Replacing " Magdyno." It is advisable, first, to remove the engine-timing cover. Then remove the h.t. lead from the sparking plug and also the dynamo leads. Referring to Fig. 59, remove the locking bolt *B* and the centre one of the three bolts *A*. Slacken the two outer bolts *A*. Now remove the Lucas "Magdyno." Replacement should be effected in the reverse order. Tightening of the bolts should be done *after* the timing cover has been replaced and the chain has been re-tensioned. Re-tensioning can be effected by moving the "Magdyno" in the required direction with the "Magdyno" security bolts slackened off.

Removal of Timing Gears and Oil Pump (1946 to 1947). First on S.V. and O.H.V. models remove the timing cover as described in a previous paragraph. Then remove the two valve rockers, which, though identical, should be not be interchanged. Examine both valve rockers for wear at the contact areas, i.e. where they ride on the cams.

Withdraw the inlet camwheel, and proceed to remove the engine pinion nut which drives the oil pump (via a worm) and has a L.H. thread. Now withdraw the exhaust camwheel and remove the oil pump from the two studs after unscrewing the two securing nuts. The engine pinion can now (not before) be extracted if necessary.

Replacing Timing Gears and Oil Pump (1946 to 1947). If new timing gears are to be fitted to a S.V. or O.H.V. engine, check both camwheels for side-float. Detach the plug covering the end of the exhaust camwheel spindle. It is pressed into the timing cover. Next replace both camwheels, and fit and secure the timing cover, tightening all nine securing screws. Then check, in turn, the side-float of the inlet and exhaust camwheel spindles. The side-float of the inlet camwheel spindle can be felt on pushing and pulling the protruding spindle sideways. With the exhaust camwheel, insert tightly a tapered piece of steel (such as the tag

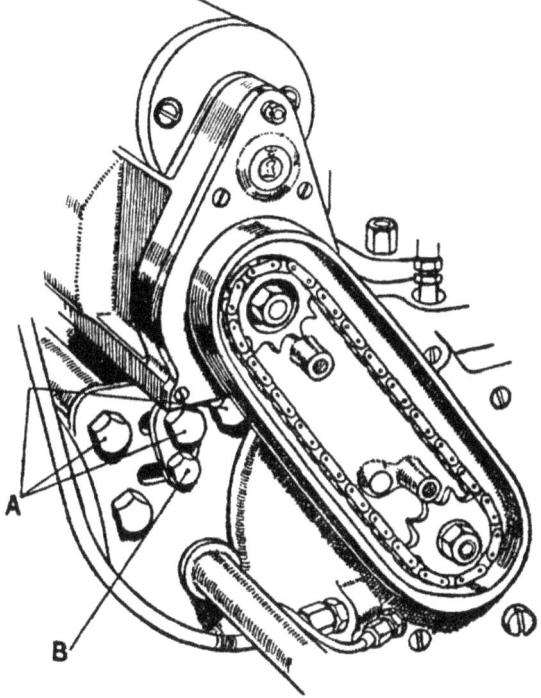

Fig. 59. Showing "Magdyno" Securing Bolts

end of a file) into the hollow camwheel spindle, and check for side-float in a similar manner. The correct side-float for both camwheels is ·004 in. Excessive side-float can be rectified by fitting pen steel washers to the camwheel spindles on each side of the camwheels. Having obtained correct side-float, remove the timing cover and press in the plug covering the end of the exhaust camwheel spindle.

Replace both rockers, and check with a feeler gauge the clearance between the face of each camwheel and the back of the corresponding rocker. The correct clearance is ·006 in. Next remove the rockers and camwheels. If the engine pinion has been removed, replace it. Put the piston at T.D.C. In this position the key for the engine pinion should be at the bottom of the main-shaft, and of the three pinion key-ways, that should be used which causes the timing mark to be in the 2 o'clock position. Fit the exhaust camwheel and then the inlet camwheel, taking care to see that the timing marks register correctly. Afterwards fit both rockers and check the valve timing (see page 105). Fit the engine pinion (and pump-driving worm) nut. Then examine and fit the oil pump, replace the timing cover, fit the "Magdyno" driving chain and sprockets, tension the chain, and finally check the ignition timing.

Where Timing Gears are Unmarked. If for some reason the timing gears are renewed and the new gears are unmarked, care must be taken to ascertain that the correct valve timing is obtained. Place the piston at T.D.C. and mesh the exhaust camwheel with the engine pinion such that the exhaust valve is about to close. Similarly, mesh the inlet camwheel such that the inlet valve is about to open. Check the timing to verify that it is correct (page 105), and then proceed to move each camwheel *one tooth* in the required direction until the correct valve timing is obtained. If difficulty is experienced in obtaining the exact timing, remove the engine pinion and replace it, using the next key-way until timing is in accordance with the specified figure. The effect of moving the engine pinion one key-way is equivalent to altering the timing by one-third of a tooth.

Inspecting and Fitting Oil Pump. Unless absolutely essential, it is not recommended that the oil pump be stripped. It is advisable, however, when the pump has been removed to test for play in the spindle by pushing and pulling the worm wheel. By rotating the spindle while covering the oil holes with the fingers, it should be possible to feel the suction effect of the pump if it is in reasonably good condition. While actuating the pump, it should also be possible to feel any obstruction caused by the presence of foreign matter. Clean the pump thoroughly with paraffin before replacing it.

It is assumed that the driving worm and nut (L.H. thread) has been fitted next to the engine pinion. Before fitting the pump itself, thoroughly clean the face to which the pump is to be fitted, and also the back of the pump. If jointing compound is used, employ only a light film and be most careful not to block up the oil holes. Examine and fit the fibre washer (see Fig. 58) between the pump feed and the timing cover.

Removing Timing Gear Bushes. On making a general overhaul, the condition of the timing gear bushes may be found such that

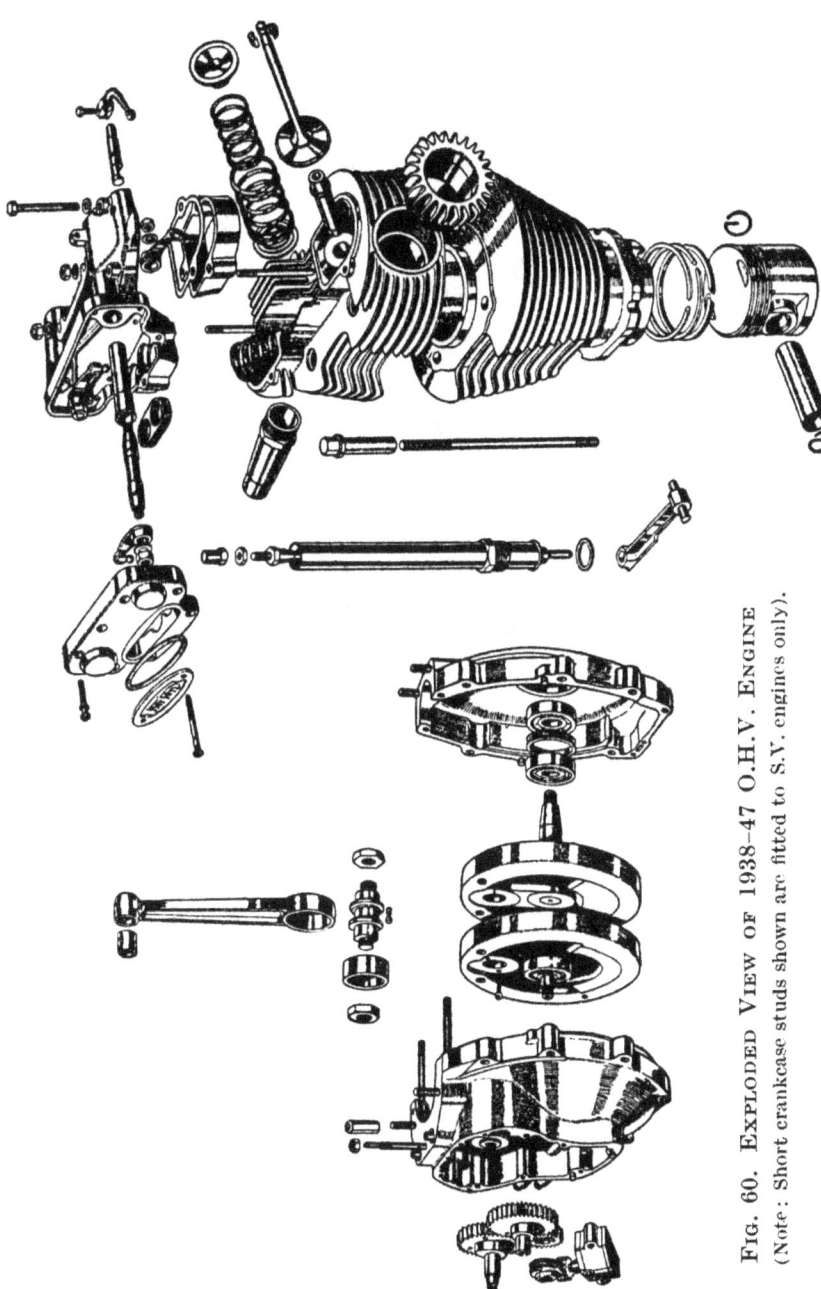

Fig. 60. Exploded View of 1938–47 O.H.V. Engine
(Note: Short crankcase studs shown are fitted to S.V. engines only).

renewal of bushes is called for. This work is best undertaken by the Norton Service Department. The timing cover and the corresponding crankcase half should be forwarded to Bracebridge Street, accompanied by a label with your address and name on it.

Removing and Fitting Petrol Tank. Petrol tank removal is advised when decarbonizing all models, with the exception of a top overhaul of the S.V. machines involving cylinder head removal only.

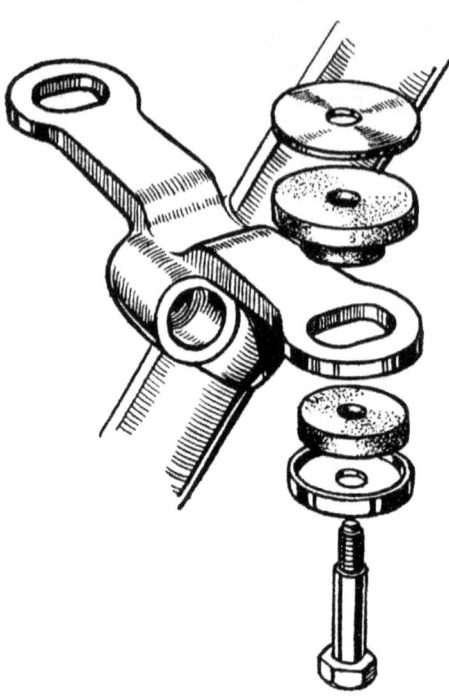

FIG. 61. CORRECT ORDER FOR ASSEMBLING FUEL TANK MOUNTING WASHERS

Draining is unnecessary, but verify that the petrol tap levers are turned to the "Off" position. In this position the round end of each lever is pressed in. Disconnect the fuel pipes from the taps, gripping the union nut with one spanner and applying a second one to the tap union. To free the petrol tank from the frame on 1938 and later models, remove the four securing bolts and washers. Four steel washers and four shouldered rubber washers will be found on each side of the two tank brackets.

To replace the petrol tank, lay the four shouldered rubber washers on the frame tank brackets, and place the four steel washers above them. Then position the petrol tank and fit the four cupped steel and the four rubber washers on to the tank securing bolts. The correct order of assembling the washers is clearly illustrated in Fig. 61. Next fit the four bolts to the tank and tighten them evenly. Verify that the tank does not at any point foul the frame, and finally replace the petrol pipes, using two spanners as for dismantling.

Removing S.V. Cylinder Head (1938 to 1947). Remove the h.t. lead from the sparking plug and the plug also. Then remove the nine nuts which secure the cylinder head to the barrel, and lift off the cylinder head and the joint washer.

APPENDIX

Note on Decarbonizing S.V. Models. When undertaking a top overhaul of a Model 16H or "Big Four," scrape off all carbon from the top of the piston and from the inside of the cylinder head, being careful not to damage the piston, which is of a light alloy. It is not advisable to remove *all* carbon from the edge of the piston crown, as this carbon forms an effective oil seal and prevents excessive oil consumption. It is a good plan to place an old piston ring at the top of the bore and resting on the piston crown, so as to mask the area from which the carbon is not to be removed. Of course, all the carbon *can* be scraped off, the only ill effect being a temporary increase in oil consumption until a new carbon seal is formed. The above remarks apply particularly to engines which have had considerable usage.

Replacing S.V. Cylinder Head (1938 to 1947). Inspect the joint washer and renew it if there is evidence of blowing. Fit this washer with its bright side *towards* the cylinder barrel. Replace the cylinder head and tighten down the nine nuts evenly. Finally replace the sparking plug and h.t. lead.

Removing S.V. Cylinder Barrel, etc. (1938 to 1947). It is possible to remove a Model 16H or "Big Four" cylinder barrel with or without the cylinder head in position. But first remove the petrol tank (see page 110) and detach the h.t. lead and sparking plug. Next remove the Amal carburettor, complete with petrol pipes, from the induction stub. Loosen the bolt on the split ring and ease off the carburettor, allowing it to be suspended from the throttle and air control cables.

Remove the cover from the valve chest and turn the engine over until the piston is at B.D.C. with both valves closed. Detach the exhaust valve lifter control from the arm (see Fig. 57) by lifting the arm and releasing the inner cable. This will free the return spring, and the cable adjuster can be unscrewed from the cylinder barrel, rendering the cable completely disconnected. Now remove from the cylinder barrel the exhaust valve lifter spindle, which is secured by a set pin in the base of the cylinder. Take out this set pin and remove the spindle, complete with oil-retaining washer and spring.

To free the cylinder barrel, remove the five nuts from the studs at its base. One of these nuts will be found *inside* the valve chest. Now carefully withdraw the cylinder barrel in the manner shown in Fig. 41. It should be noted that a paper washer is interposed between the crankcase and the cylinder barrel; also that it is not necessary to remove the valve guide lubricator shown in Fig. 57. Cover up the mouth of the crankcase with a large clean cloth to prevent any foreign matter entering the crankcase. Then proceed with piston removal. To do this, remove *one* circlip and push out the gudgeon-pin, which is a running fit in the small-end bush. Mark the piston to ensure correct replacement, and scrap the circlip which has been removed.

Removing O.H.V. Rocker-box, Cylinder Head, Cylinder Barrel, etc. (1938 to 1947).

Remove the petrol tank (see page 110). Also remove the Amal carburettor, with petrol pipes, from the induction stub, after first loosening the bolt on the split ring. Take off the exhaust pipe, or detach the complete exhaust system as a unit.

Turn the engine over until both valves are closed, and remove the sparking plug and rocker adjustment inspection cover. Next remove the rocker-box cover, the rocker-box securing bolts and nuts, the rocker-box itself, and the two distance pieces. These and other components are clearly shown in Fig. 60, which shows an exploded view of the 1938-47 O.H.V. engine.

Detach both push-rods and cover tubes, being careful not to mix up the inlet and exhaust members. Unscrew the four cylinder head nuts, leaving the rocker-box hanging from the exhaust valve lifter cable, or, alternatively, remove completely. Withdraw the cylinder head from the cylinder barrel spigot. The cylinder barrel itself need not be removed every time the engine is decarbonized, as the top of the piston can be scraped clean as on the S.V. models (see page 111).

If it is desired to remove the cylinder barrel also in order to examine the piston and piston rings, turn the engine over until the piston is at B.D.C. and lift the barrel off vertically (see Fig. 41), while supporting the piston with the hand. Cover up the mouth of the crankcase with a cloth, and proceed to remove the piston by taking out *one* circlip and pushing out the fully floating gudgeon-pin. Mark the piston to ensure correct replacement. Decarbonize thoroughly (see page 79). If it is decided not to fit new piston rings, it is best not to disturb the carbon which has probably formed at the backs of the rings. The removal and inspection of piston rings are dealt with on page 78. Valve grinding is dealt with on page 81.

Dismantling O.H.V. Rocker-box (1938 to 1947).

When the rocker-box has been removed from the engine, check the rocker assembly for wear and end float of the bushes and spindles. Remove the valve rocker arm nut and washer, and remove the rocker arm by lightly tapping the arm off the spindle taper. Then withdraw the spindle and push-rod arm from the rocker-box. Next remove the push-rod arm.

There should be no perceptible end float in the rocker spindle

APPENDIX 113

assembly. Excessive end float can be remedied by fitting shims obtainable from the Service Department of Norton Motors, Ltd.

A worn rocker bush can be extracted in the manner shown in Fig. 62, which is self-explanatory. New bushes should be pressed in, or tapped home with a hammer and wooden block. After fitting a new bush, see that the necessary oil holes are drilled.

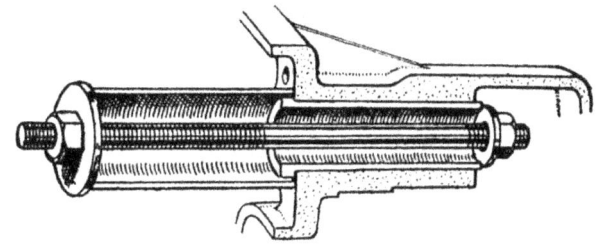

FIG. 62. METHOD OF EXTRACTING ROCKER ARM BUSH

To detach the exhaust valve lifter, remove the cable from the arm. Then take out the securing pin in the top of the rocker-box and withdraw the valve lifter, complete with the arm.

Should it be necessary to renew a rocker ball end or a valve rocker pad, it may readily be knocked out.

Valves and Valve Guides. See that all carbon is removed from the under sides of the valve heads, but do not polish the valve stems. Always grind-in the valves when fitting *new* valves, but do not grind-in used valves unless they are seating badly. If the valves or their seats are badly burnt or pitted, it may be impossible to obtain good results by grinding-in (see page 81), and the remedy is to have the seats re-cut and the valves re-faced.

Both valve guides are a driving fit in the cylinder head or cylinder barrel and, to remove, tap them out with a double diameter drift. Removal, however, is only necessary if excessive clearance between the valves and guides has developed through wear. Use the above-mentioned drift to fit new guides or replace old ones. After fitting valve guides, it is generally necessary to true up the valve seats with a cutter to ensure that the seats and guides are in true alignment.

Replacing the Valves. Clean very thoroughly the valve seats, valves, and pockets. Replace the valve springs and collars, and oil the valve stems. Insert the valves in their guides, compress the valve springs, and replace the split cotters. Greasing the latter will facilitate assembly while the springs are being compressed.

The Piston. The correct piston ring gaps are specified on page 78. The side clearance, measured with a feeler, of the rings in their grooves should be ·002 in. Check the rings in the cylinder bore for gap by placing each ring in the bore and pushing it down square by means of the piston.

The correct piston clearances (at the top of skirt) are for Model 16H, ·0067 in. to ·0057 in.; for Model 1, ·0075 in. to ·0065 in.; for Models 18 and ES2, ·0085 in. to ·0075 in.

When replacing the piston, fit the piston to the connecting-rod in the same position as before and fit a *new* circlip. Then proceed to fit the cylinder barrel.

Replacing S.V. Cylinder Barrel, etc. (1938 to 1947). It is assumed that the piston rings are positioned on the piston with their gaps spaced equally apart. Oil the piston, rings, and cylinder bore. Then turn the engine until the connecting-rod big-end bearing is near its highest position, with the piston and connecting-rod pointing towards the front frame tube.

Replace the paper washer over the crankcase mouth and make certain that it does not obstruct the oil feed hole to the rear of the cylinder. Now fit the cylinder barrel over the piston, being careful to keep it square with the piston. Ease the barrel down over the piston while compressing the rings by hand. Assistance may be needed. Then tighten the cylinder base securing nuts firmly and evenly.

Next fit the exhaust valve lifter spindle to the cylinder barrel, complete with felt washer and spring. Place the milled end under the collar of the exhaust tappet, so that when the spindle is turned, the tappet is raised. To secure the spindle, replace the set pin. Afterwards fit the exhaust valve lifter cable adjuster to the cylinder, and also the return spring. Fit the exhaust valve lifter cable to the actuating arm, and finally adjust the inlet and exhaust tappets to give the correct valve clearances. (See page 61.)

Replacing O.H.V. Cylinder Barrel, Cylinder Head, Rocker-box, etc. (1938 to 1947). Verify that the piston ring gaps are equally spaced, and oil the rings, piston, and the bore of the cylinder barrel. Next rotate the engine until the piston and big-end are near T.D.C., with the connecting-rod and piston pointing towards the front frame tube. Fit the paper washer over the mouth of the crankcase, being careful to see that the oil hole on the crankcase face is not masked.

Using assistance if necessary, ease the cylinder barrel over the piston, and slide it down the piston and barrel-fixing studs (see Fig. 42). Push the cylinder barrel right home.

Next, clean the cylinder barrel and cylinder head joint faces. If no joint washer is specified, smear the contacting faces with some oil. If a joint washer is provided, replace it. Then replace the cylinder head itself, fit the retaining nuts, and tighten the latter firmly and evenly.

Fit the two rocker-box distance pieces on the cylinder head (see Fig. 60) and fit paper washers on the distance pieces. No washers are required between the distance pieces and the cylinder head. Now fit the rocker-box itself and its retaining bolts and nuts. Tighten the nuts evenly and securely.

Having replaced the rocker-box, proceed to replace the two push-rods and push-rod cover tubes in precisely their former position. Be very careful to see that the rubber oil seal is properly fitted to the rocker-box. Then fit the rocker-box cover, taking special care to see that no rubber is trapped between the joint faces of the rocker-box and the cover. If the exhaust valve lifter cable has been disconnected at the rocker-box, reconnect it. Finally adjust the push-rods to give the correct valve clearances (see page 61), and replace the petrol tank as described on page 110.

Removing Engine from Cradle Frame. Complete removal of the engine from the cradle frame, used on all post-war Nortons and some pre-war models, is advisable when undertaking a very thorough overhaul. This presents no great difficulty. First, remove the petrol tank (see page 110), take off the "Magdyno" (see page 106), and disconnect the exhaust valve lifter cable. Then remove as a unit the Amal carburettor. If desired, this may be left attached to the control cables. With the "C" spanner provided in the tool kit, undo the locking ring (on O.H.V. models) which secures the exhaust pipe to the exhaust port. Remove completely the exhaust pipe and the silencer. By undoing the clip bolts and nuts, the exhaust pipe and silencer can be removed together, instead of separately.

Disconnect at the crankcase the delivery and return pipes leading to the oil tank. If the latter has not been drained, plug the end of the delivery pipe. Remove the oil-bath chain case, the engine sprocket, and also the clutch. Take off the front and rear engine plates, remove the engine cradle bolts, and lift the engine right out of the cradle frame.

Fitting Engine to Cradle Frame. Proceed in the reverse order of dismantling. Carefully lift the engine into the cradle, and insert both cradle bolts. Beginning at the rear engine plates fit all bolts loosely and work round to the front engine plate bolt. Afterwards tighten all securing nuts firmly. Complete the assembly by replacing the clutch, engine sprocket, oil-bath chain case, etc. Replace the Lucas "Magdyno" (see page 106) and time it correctly (see page 88). Finally reconnect the oil pipes, and fit the exhaust system, carburettor, and petrol tank.

Inspecting Connecting-rod Bearings. Both the big-end and the small-end bearings can be inspected for wear when the cylinder barrel is taken off the engine. To examine the condition of the big-end bearing, turn the flywheels until the big-end is at T.D.C. Then grip the connecting-rod with *both* hands, and push and pull it in a vertical direction. Be careful not to exert any side pressure, as some end float is permissible. A small amount of up-and-down movement is acceptable, but appreciable "rock" indicates excessive wear, and a new crankpin bearing is called for. This necessitates parting the crankcase halves and the dismantling of the flywheel assembly. The former is a job which can be undertaken readily; but the latter, and the fitting of a new big-end bearing (and subsequent aligning of the flywheels), is a job best undertaken by the makers, who have the necessary jigs and tools available. The same applies to the small-end bearing.

After a new small-end bush is fitted, it requires to be reamed to fit the gudgeon-pin, and drilling the oil holes is necessary. Those with good workshop facilities and experience can tackle the work, but, as with the big-end bearing, it is generally best to entrust the job to the engine manufacturer. The gudgeon-pin should be a good running fit in both the small-end bush and the piston bosses. By attempting to rock the gudgeon-pin in its bush, play can readily be detected.

Splitting the Crankcase. First drain off all oil in the sump by removing the drain plug. Then remove the cylinder barrel, piston, timing gears, and oil pump. Remove the key from the engine driving mainshaft. Undo all the crankcase external nuts and tap out the bolts. Also remove the cheese-headed screw from the oil sump. It is now possible to begin splitting the crankcase.

If the crankcase halves do not readily separate, some leverage is necessary. Turn the flywheels until the crankpin is near the mouth of the crankcase, and lever the timing side half off by resting a lever against the crankpin nut and applying outward leverage.

To remove the driving side half of the crankcase, lightly drop the end of the driving shaft on to a block of hard wood, when

APPENDIX

the crankcase half should part from the shaft. Considerable care is required when fitting the flywheel assembly to the crankcase and bolting the two halves together. For this reason the author advocates that when big end trouble develops, the complete flywheel *and* crankcase assembly be sent to the Norton Service Department at Bracebridge Street, Birmingham, 29, for their expert attention. If you have sufficient confidence, split the crankcase, forward the flywheel assembly only, and reassemble the crankcase yourself.

Assembling the Crankcase. Fit the flywheel assembly temporarily into the crankcase, and secure the crankcase halves by fitting and tightening *all* bolts. Then check the flywheels for correct end float (·005 in.). If end float is found excessive, take out the flywheel assembly and fit pen steel washers as required to both mainshafts. To ensure central disposition of the flywheels in the crankcase, be sure to fit the same thickness of washers on each side. Replace the flywheel assembly, bolt up the crankcase, and again check the end float.

Next check that the connecting-rod is quite central in the crankcase, taking into account connecting-rod end float. Grip the base of the connecting-rod and push it towards the timing side as far as possible. Then measure the distance between the mouth of the crankcase and the end of the small-end bush on the timing side. Similarly push the connecting-rod hard over to the driving side and record the same measurement on this side. The difference between the two measurements should not exceed $\frac{1}{64}$ in. To make an adjustment for alignment, transfer pen steel washers from one side to the other as required. After obtaining correct alignment, remove the flywheel assembly from the crankcase and proceed with the final assembly.

Oil the big-end and mainshaft bearings. Then smear some jointing compound or gold size on the two edges of the crankcase halves. Fit the flywheel assembly into the crankcase and bolt up the latter. Replace the timing gears and oil pump, also the timing cover (see page 106). After fitting the cylinder, etc., check the valve timing.

If the valve stem lubricator has been removed from the crankcase of a S.V. engine (see Fig. 57), replace this. Screw the lubricator home and check that the oil holes point *towards the valve stems*. The bevelled side must face towards the cylinder.

1946-7 Clutch Adjustment. It should normally be done by means of the cable adjuster in the top rear corner of the gearbox end cover. A further adjustment, where necessary, should be made by removing the sprung-in cover in the centre of the gearbox outer cover, slackening the clutch operating arm securing pin, and then rotating the clutch worm as required. To do this, insert the blade of a screwdriver in the slot across the end of the clutch worm shank, while holding the clutch operating arm.

Fork Spindle Adjustment. An identical method of adjustment is used for the two top spindles and the bottom rear spindle. First the lock-nuts at each end of the spindle should be slackened. The spindle should then be rotated *anti-clockwise* by means of a spanner applied to its squared end, until the spindle is just tight. Then slacken back about half a turn and tighten up the lock-nuts. To adjust the bottom front spindle, first unscrew the shock-absorber knob until the star washer behind is just free. Then slacken the lock-nut and rotate the spindle *clockwise* until just tight. The spindle should then be slackened back about half a turn and the lock-nut re-tightened. Finally check for free fork action. Telescopic forks are dealt with on page 124.

To Dismantle Spring Frame. Dismantling should not be necessary until after a very considerable mileage when some dust may be found to have penetrated past the telescopic covers. To dismantle the mechanism for inspection, cleaning or spring renewal, proceed as follows.

Remove the rear wheel complete. Next loosen the clip pin across the top of the rear frame member which secures the stationary plunger rod. Then unscrew four or five turns the locking pin at the bottom of the rear frame member and with a mallet or soft hammer tap out the pin. This frees the stationary plunger from its taper. Now remove completely the bottom locking pin and withdraw upwards the stationary plunger from the frame member. Having done this, insert a tyre lever at the side of the top and bottom covers and between the covers and the frame, as far as possible towards the top and the bottom. A little leverage should now suffice to force the covers away from the frame member and enable the complete assembly to be removed and dealt with. To prevent the springs flying out when removing the assembly, it is a good plan when enough of the central hole is exposed to insert a $\frac{5}{16}$ in. diameter bar threaded at both ends and fitted with large wing nuts.

To Reassemble. After thoroughly inspecting and cleaning the various parts, smear a little oil on the fork end bearing surface and replace the springs and covers in position on the fork end. See that the stronger spring is refitted at the top. Now reinsert the assembly into the jaw of the rear frame member. This may be rather difficult unless the springs are first compressed to occupy

APPENDIX 119

a space slightly less than that of the rear frame member. To overcome the difficulty, use the bar referred to above for dismantling. After positioning the spring assembly into the rear member jaw, remove the bar and fit the assembly into its approximate position. Smear the stationary plunger with oil, insert the

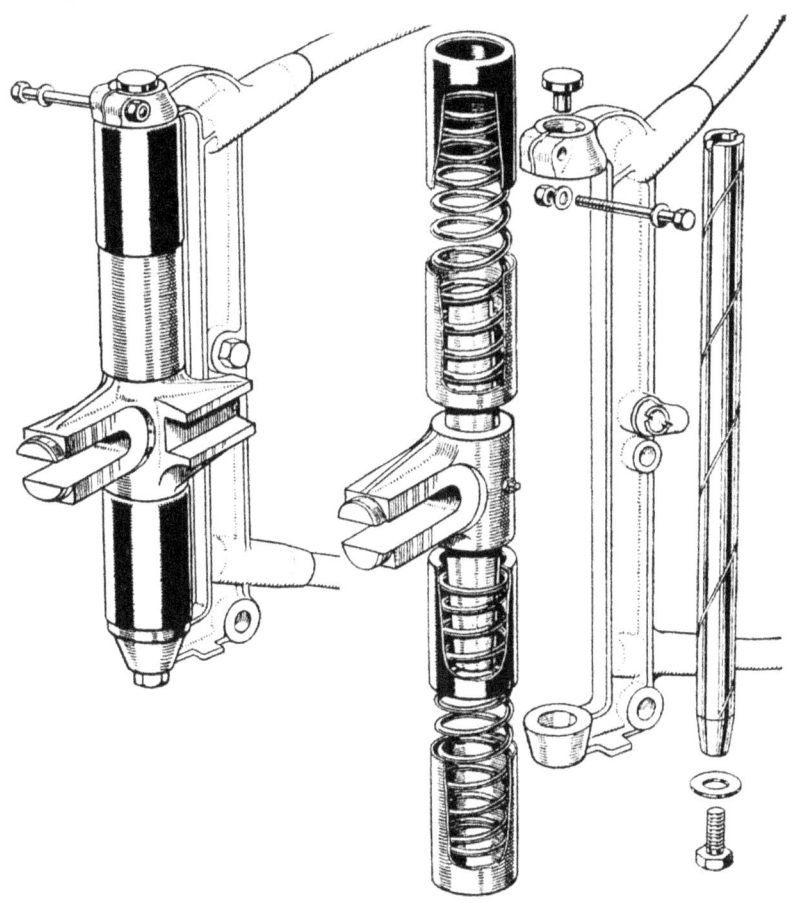

FIG. 63. SPRING FRAME

taper end first into the upper hole in the rear member. It should not be difficult to push the plunger home because the tapered end readily draws the cups into correct alinement. Finally replace the bottom locking pin and tighten the top clip pin.

Be careful when replacing the rear wheel to see that the fork ends are as nearly parallel with each other as possible and that the open end of the jaw faces to the rear. Also when adjusting the secondary chain (page 69) avoid letting the rear wheel be moved farther along the fork end away from the plunger than is absolutely necessary, otherwise the wheel spindle may be unduly stressed. If a big chain adjustment is necessary, remove a link.

Instructions for Dismantling 1946-7 Gearbox. The four-speed gearbox can be stripped down in the following way. First remove the kick-starter crank, gear indicator, and the gear lever. Next remove the gearbox outer cover and release the clutch cable from the clutch arm. Having done this, remove the cable adjuster from the inner cover. Also remove the split cotter and pin from the jaw joint on the gear control rod. Now unscrew the nuts holding the inner end cover to the gearbox. Take off the complete end cover. Remove the kick-starter axle return spring and the cover from the bush and withdraw the kick-starter axle from the cover. Take out the kick-starter pawl pin from the kick-starter axle and withdraw the pawl, plunger, and spring.

If the clutch has already been taken off the mainshaft, place a length of tubing over the mainshaft and secure it with the clutch retaining nut. This will enable the gears to be removed from the gearbox casing without disturbing the mainshaft. Proceed to remove the low gear pinion and kick-starter wheel, also the second gear from the main axle. Unscrew the operating fork shaft from the gearbox and remove the layshaft second gear and operating fork. Remove the main axle, third gear, and the associated operating fork. Take out the layshaft with its two remaining gears. This will withdraw the inner race of the layshaft roller bearing, leaving the outer race in the gearbox.

Detach the tubular distance piece fitted to the clutch end of the main axle and withdraw carefully. The rollers in the main gear wheel, in which the main axle runs, are now left in position. It is advisable to employ a rolled piece of card to retain them until the mainshaft is replaced. To remove the main gear wheel, where necessary, remove the gearbox sprocket nut (L.H. thread) and the sprocket. Afterwards withdraw the main gear wheel from the gearbox, together with the rollers.

Repairing GR-S Synthetic Tyre Tubes. These tubes may readily be identified by means of a 1 in. diameter red disc near the valve, or by means of a stripe round the base of the tube. Use the same material for repairs as for repairing tubes made of genuine rubber. Although it is practicable to effect an emergency repair of nail holes and injuries up to $\frac{1}{4}$ in., it is preferable to have the damage put right by vulcanizing. Where the injury exceeds

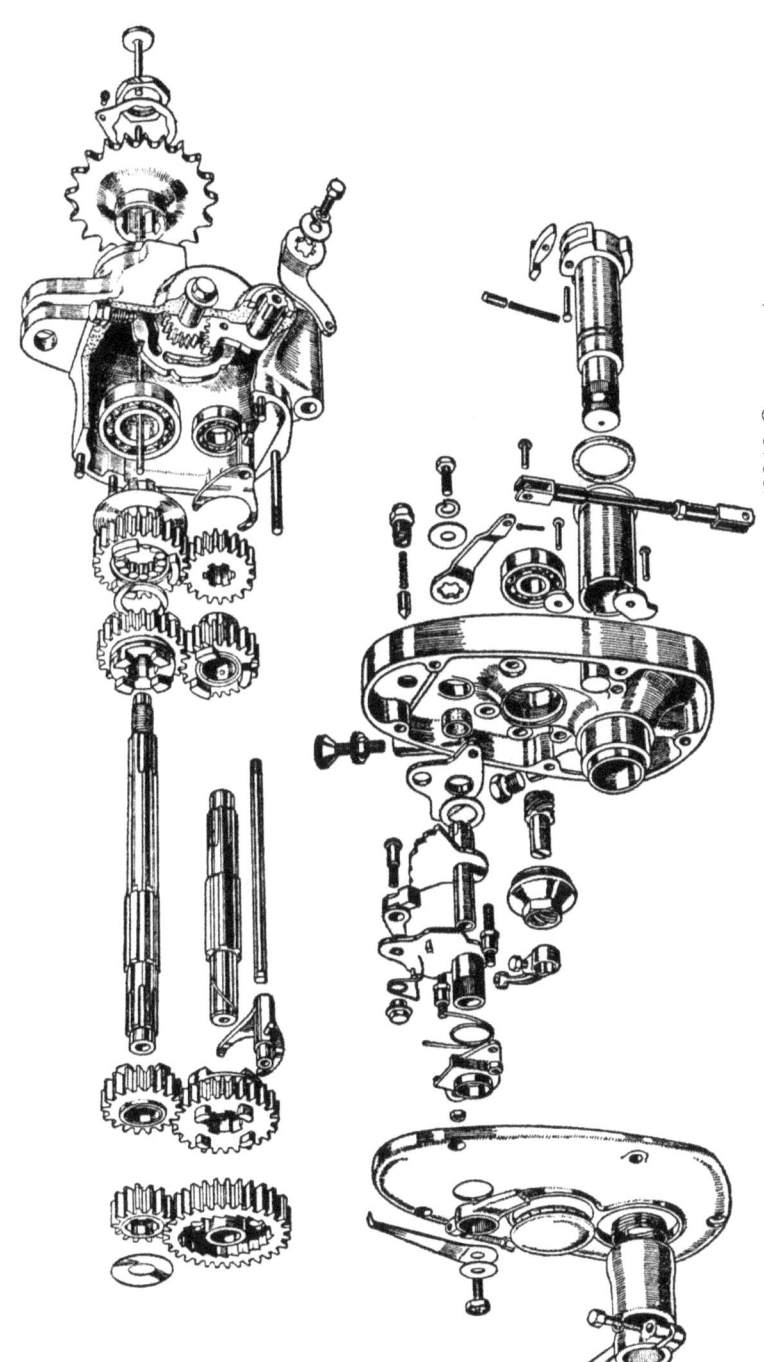

Fig. 64. Exploded View of Norton Gearbox (1946 Onwards)

$\frac{1}{4}$ in., it is always wise to have a proper vulcanized repair. If you effect emergency repairs, note the following important points—

(a) Roughen the surface of the tube around the injury for an area slightly larger than the patch to be affixed. Use sand-paper or a wire brush to remove all surface glaze, and afterwards rub off all traces of dust.

(b) Choose a suitable size patch not smaller than $1\frac{1}{2}$ in. diameter, and take off the linen backing. An excellent type of patch is the Dunlop "Vulcafix."

(c) Apply one coat of solution to the tube and before applying the patch, allow the solution to dry thoroughly.

(d) Apply the patch and press it firmly down with the fingers. Afterwards dust the repaired area thoroughly with french chalk.

Repairing Non-synthetic Tyres. Dunlop auto-vulcanizing patches, such as "Vulcafix," are equally suitable for repairing non-synthetic rubber tubes as those made from the "imitation" rubber. Clean the tube thoroughly with sandpaper and rub off all dust. Then select a suitable patch and detach the linen backing by stretching the rubber. The patch can be affixed with or without solution. If using solution, apply *to the tube only* and wait until it becomes "tacky." If not using solution, rub the prepared face of the patch with a cloth moistened with petrol and transfer the brown deposit on the cloth to the tube. Repeat this operation, and allow one minute for the patch and transferred deposit to dry. Apply the patch to the tube, using slight pressure, especially around the edges. Now affix the patch to the tube. It should become automatically vulcanized.

Care of Synthetic Tyres. Tyres made of synthetic rubber instead of natural rubber are more prone to injury and require greater care. Check the inflation pressures at least once a week (see page 21), and avoid excessive speed and fierce acceleration. To obtain maximum life, inspect the cover frequently for cuts and tears. Also, after effecting a tube repair, take special precautions when replacing the tube. The procedure advised by the Dunlop Co. is as follows:

Dust the inside of the cover evenly with french chalk. Then pump up the tube until it assumes a rounded form. Then insert it in the cover. Now apply a frothy solution of soap and water liberally around the entire base of the tube, extending upwards between the tyre beads and the tube itself for at least 2 in. on both sides. Apply the frothy solution also to the bottom and outside of the tyre beads. Do not permit any solution to run into the crown of the tyre. The solution should be such as to feel slippery when the fingers are wetted and rubbed together.

Mount the tyre on the rim immediately while the soap solution is still wet, and before inflating the tube, check that the cover beads are clear of the rim right round. Inflate the tyre fully until all beads are seated fully. Then deflate the tube completely and re-inflate to the correct pressure. The object of a second

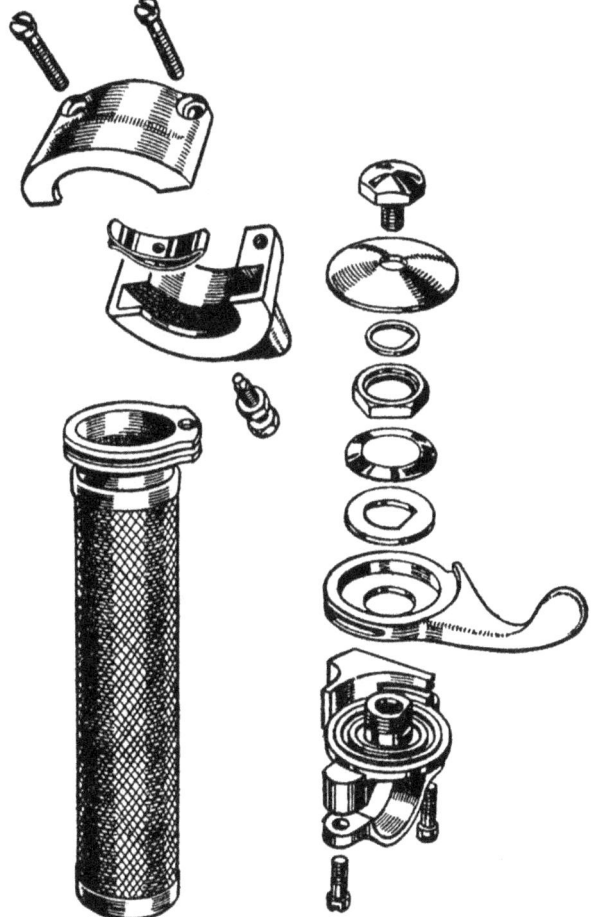

FIG. 65. COMPONENTS OF TWIST-GRIP AND AIR LEVER
The ignition lever assembly is the same as the air lever

inflation is to permit any stretched parts of the tube to re-adjust themselves in the cover and to prevent the tube becoming strained. French chalk can be used as a substitute for soap solution, but this is not desirable. The repair of synthetic tyres is dealt with on page 120.

Assembling and Dismantling Twist-grip. Grease that portion of the handlebars on which the grip operates. Referring to Fig. 65, fit the sleeve to the bar. Apply some grease to the drum on the sleeve. Then fit the spring and adjuster bolt and nut to the lower half clip. Pass the control cable through the clip hole and fit the nipple to the drum on the sleeve. Assemble the upper half clip and adjust the twist-grip for tightness by means of the adjusting screw, afterwards locking it in the desired position. To dismantle the twist-grip, proceed in the reverse order of assembling.

Steering Head Adjustment (Telescopic Forks). Raise the front wheel clear of the ground by placing a suitable box under the engine cradle. Then place the thumb of the left hand on the joint between the steering head and the fork head clip. Endeavour to lift the front forks with the right hand, when any play in the steering head races should easily be detected.

If an adjustment is needed, slacken the steering column locking nut, and also the pinch bolt which clamps each fork leg to the fork crown. Remove steering head slackness by adjusting the nut on the steering column below the head clip. Make sure that the telescopic forks are quite free to rotate on the head races and, when the required adjustment has been made, re-tighten the steering column locking nut and the two pinch bolts.

Removing Telescopic Forks from Frame. The front wheel and mudguard can, if desired, be left in position. First detach the switch panel from the headlamp and remove the steering damper arm from the frame. Also disconnect the speedometer lighting and driving cables from the speedometer head. Disconnect all control cables from the handlebars and remove the latter. Now completely slacken the steering damper, and remove the steering column locking nut, complete with damper rod and knob. Next take off the oil filler plugs and the speedometer panel. Remove the steering head clip and adjusting nut. Then withdraw the telescopic forks, being careful not to lose any balls from the steering head races. Also avoid spilling any damping oil from the fork legs. If this happens, subsequent replenishment (see page 102) will be necessary.

Fitting Telescopic Forks to Frame. First inspect the steering-head races and balls. There should be 17 balls per race. If the races are pitted, knock them out of their housings and renew. With regard to the races in the frame, each has a small hole provided to permit the entry of grease. See that this is clear. Grease generously the track of the race fitted to the base of the steering column, and the top frame race. Position the 34 balls and gently insert the steering column through the frame head.

Position the top race and dust cover, and then screw the adjusting nut down the column until the hexagon is bearing against the top race lightly. Now replace the steering head clip and the speedometer panel. Also fit loosely the steering column locking nut, and fit and tighten firmly both filler plugs. Afterwards adjust the steering head correctly, replace the remaining items, and check all nuts and bolts for security.

Dismantling Telescopic Fork Legs. Fig. 66 shows the "innards" of each fork leg, which can be dismantled with the forks fitted to the frame, or removed. A "pull through" may be required to remove and replace the main tube. Dismantle each leg in the following manner:

First remove the front wheel and mudguard. Remove the damping oil filler, and drain plugs from the top and bottom of each fork leg, and drain off the whole of the damping oil. Now slacken the pinch bolt in the crown lug and proceed to withdraw the fork end, complete with bottom cover, springs, and main tube. To facilitate withdrawing the main tube, screw the "pull through" into the top end, and tap out with a small mallet.

Remove the top leather washer from the main tube, also the short buffer spring and main spring. Detach the bottom cover, which is held to the fork end by a pair of screws. Take off the leather washer and then remove the locking ring from the top of the fork end. Now draw the fork end off the main tube, and dismantle the few remaining components from the tube.

Assembling Telescopic Forks. Clean carefully all the members comprising each fork leg, and renew worn parts as required. Then secure the bottom bush to the main tube by means of the retaining nut. Position the fork end on the main tube. Next assemble the shouldered bush into the fork end and fit the super oil seal, making quite sure that the radiused side of the leather is at the top. Tighten the locking ring so as to be secure, but such that no distortion of the super oil seal case occurs. Replace the smaller of the two leather washers over the locking ring. Then fit the main spring, the buffer spring, and the second leather washer.

Fit the bottom cover and securing screws. Now screw the "pull through" into the top end of the main tube, and pass through the crown lug and the steering head clip. With a tommy-bar inserted across the "pull through," draw the main tube into position. Tighten the pinch bolt in the crown lug temporarily. Afterwards withdraw the "pull through," fit the filler plug to the

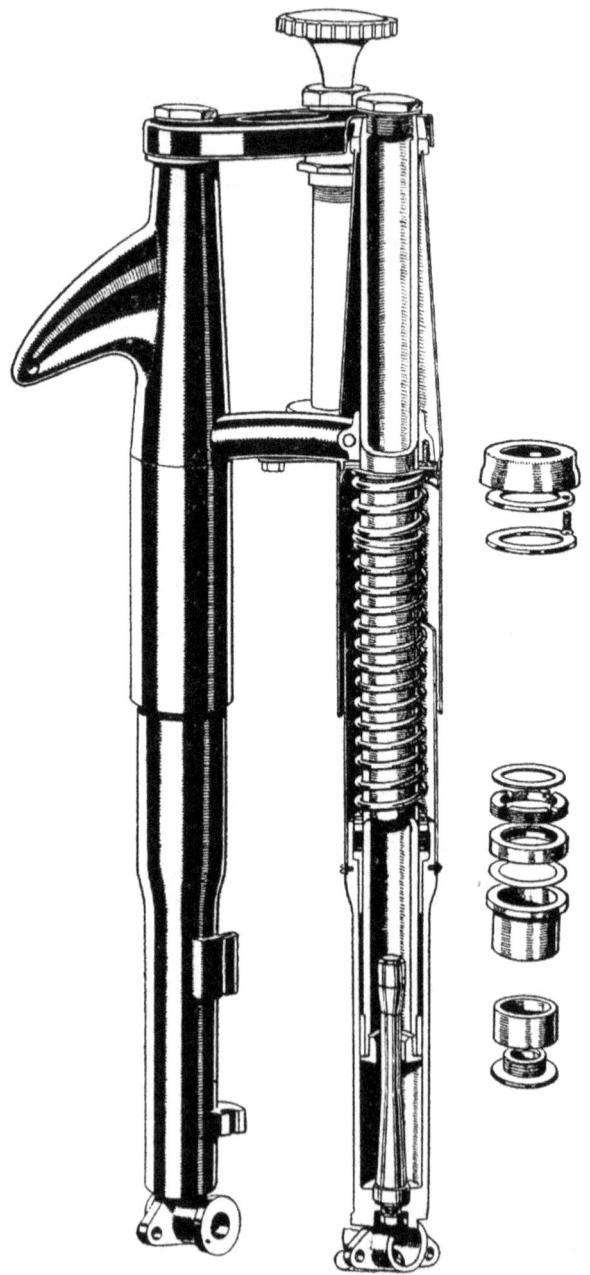

Fig. 66. Telescopic Forks (1947 onwards)

APPENDIX

main tube, and loosen the pinch bolt. Lock the main tube with the filler plug and re-tighten the pinch bolt. Finally replace the drain plug, remove the filler plug, and replenish the fork leg with damping oil. (See page 102.)

To Remove Oil-bath (1946–47). First remove the footrests, footrest rod, and the rear brake pedal. Then remove the large nut which secures the outer portion of the oil-bath, and detach the latter. Next remove the clutch spring screws, the clutch

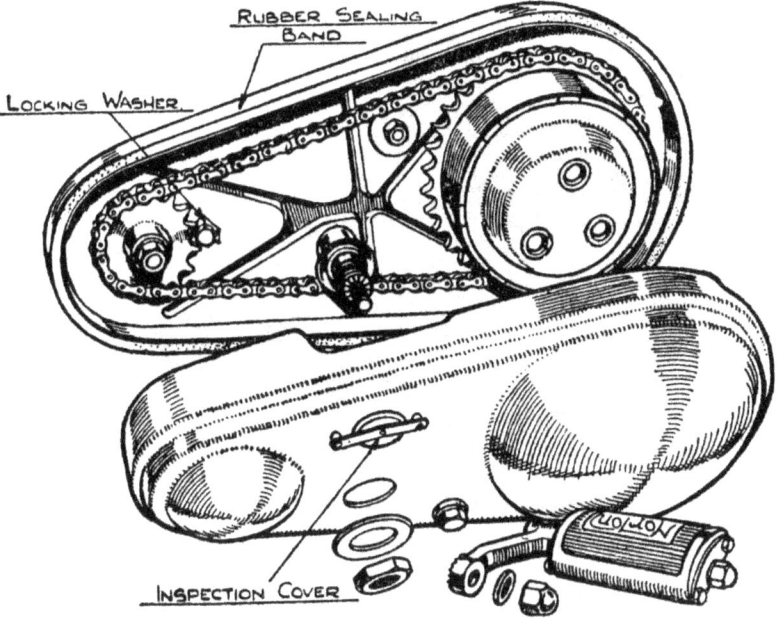

FIG. 67. OIL-BATH WITH COVER REMOVED (1946 ONWARDS)

springs, and the cups. Each of these members is in triplicate. Also remove the clutch outer plate, the clutch thrust pin, and the clutch retaining nut. While unscrewing this nut, depress the foot change until first gear is obtained and grip the rear wheel. After removing the retaining nut, withdraw the clutch body, to do which a special tool is available if necessary.

With a claw type extractor, proceed to remove the engine sprocket. Having done this, remove together the engine sprocket, clutch, and primary chain. Finally remove the inner portion of the oil-bath, which is secured by three bolts and two nuts. The inner portion of the oil-bath is secured to the crankcase by a bolt, to the engine plate by a nut, to the secondary chain guard by a bolt, and to the gearbox pivot bolt by a nut.

To Replace Oil-bath (1946-47). Assemble the oil-bath in the reverse order to that used for removal. Inspect the rubber washer fitted to the flange of the inner portion. This constitutes the oil seal, and must be in sound condition to prevent oil leakage. After assembly is completed, replenish the oil-bath with engine oil (see page 44) to the level of the plug situated close to the bottom of the outer portion of the oil-bath.

Dismantling Clutch (1946 Onwards). First remove the outer

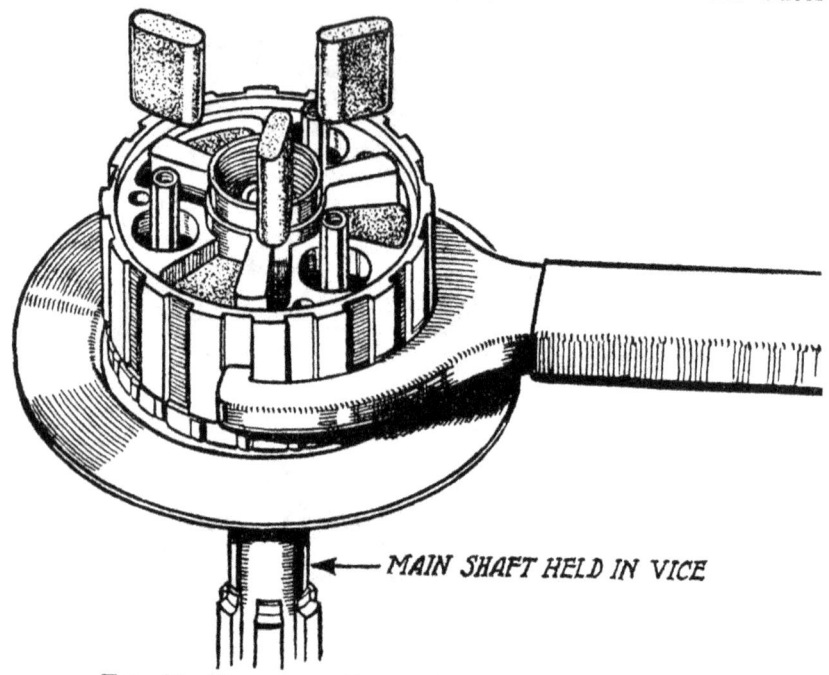

Fig. 68. Removing Shock Absorber Rubbers from Clutch Body

portion of the oil-bath. Also remove the clutch body (see appropriate instructions). If it is desired to inspect the driving slots in the clutch sprocket, it is necessary to remove the steel band which is pressed round the clutch sprocket. But if it is the rider's intention to dismantle the clutch plates only, it is permissible to leave this band in position. Its function, incidentally, is to prevent excessive oil getting on the plates.

To remove the clutch plates, detach the circlip which holds the plates on to the clutch body and withdraw the plates. It will be observed that they comprise six plain steel plates, and five steel plates with Ferodo inserts. Now remove the clutch sprocket.

Referring to Fig. 68, grip an old gearbox main axle (if to hand) between the jaws of a vice, with the splined end above the jaws, and fit the clutch body to the axle. Remove all three screws holding the front cover plate. Now remove the clutch cover plate and the shock absorber rubbers (see Fig. 68). Remove the rubbers with a large "C" spanner. Place the spanner over the body so as to engage the splines as illustrated. Compress the large rubbers while removing the smaller ones. The length of the spanner should be such that the load can be taken by the operator's thighs, while both hands are free to remove the shock absorber rubbers. A good substitute for a "C" spanner is an old plain steel clutch plate with handle attached. To remove the large and smaller rubbers, it is advisable to use a small, sharp-pointed tool.

Remove the clutch body from the axle and replace in the reverse position. Then remove the three nuts from the studs of the back cover plate. Then separate the back plate, roller race, back cover, and clutch body.

Assembling Clutch (1946 Onwards). Assemble the clutch body cover plate to the body. Check that the mating holes are in alignment and the spring studs an easy fit. Replace the clutch body centre and fit the large shock absorber rubbers. Compress these and fit the smaller ones. Replace the clutch body front cover and tighten the screws. Fit the roller race on to the back cover plate and replace the back plate spring studs. Fit nuts to the studs and tighten them, finally locking the nuts with a centre punch. Test the roller race for freeness on its track.

Replace the steel band on the sprocket, making sure that the latter does not become distorted. Check all clutch plates for free movement and fit the clutch sprocket to the body. Rotate the sprocket on the race to verify free running. Next assemble the clutch plates on the sprocket and body. The correct order of fitting is: plain steel; inserts; plain, etc. The bevelled edges of the plates must be *towards* the sprocket. Turn the sprocket to see whether the plates are free.

Fit the plate retaining circlip and assemble the clutch to the gearbox main shaft. Replace the clutch thrust pin, clutch outer plate, spring cups, springs, and spring pins. Tighten the latter fully, and then complete the assembly by replacing the outer portion of the oil-bath.

Dismantling Foot Gear Change (1946 Onwards). First remove the gearbox outer end cover, and remove the return spring cover plate, which is secured by two nuts. Detach the return spring, and remove the pawl carrier by sliding it off the ratchet plate spindle, complete with the pawls and pawl spring.

Remove the ratchet lever. A bolt with a spring and plain washer secures the lever to the back of the control box. Now remove the ratchet plate, which has a plain steel washer behind it. Remove the ratchet plunger at the back of the control box by removing the domed nut and releasing the plunger and spring. Remove the two nuts at the back of the box locking the pawl carrier stop studs.

Remove the pawl carrier stop studs and also the cam plate. Then remove the pawls from the pawl carrier by removing the sleeve nut on the pawl pin. Hold the end of the pawl pin with a screwdriver while unscrewing the nut. The pawls and return spring are now quite free.

Assembling Foot Gear Change (1946 Onwards). Assemble the spring and pawls to the pawl carrier. See that the pawls are free to move after tightening the nut. Position the cam plate and fit the two carrier stops securing the cam plate. Fit the carrier stop stud lock-nuts at the back of the box and fit the ratchet plate. Also fit the splined end of the spindle through the bush in the cam plate, and the steel washer between the ratchet and box. Assemble the felt washer on to the splined end of the shaft and into the boss on the back of the control box. With fourth gear engaged, fit the ratchet lever as high as possible.

Fit the remaining bolt and washers. See that the spring washer is next to the bolt head. Assemble the plunger and spring. Replace the pawl carrier, complete with pawls. The latter may be sprung into position with the assistance of a screwdriver. Fit the cover for the return spring, the two nuts, and grease as required. Replace the outer cover, gear change lever, and indicator. Finally fit the kick-starter crank.

Removing Front Wheel (1946 Onwards). Place the Norton on both stands and disconnect the front brake cable from the cam lever. Also disconnect the cable adjuster from the brake plate. Remove the off-side wheel spindle nut, and loosen the pinch bolt in the near-side fork end. With the left hand, support the front wheel and withdraw the spindle, using a tommy-bar inserted through the hole in the spindle head.

Fitting Front Wheel (1946 Onwards). Follow the reverse order of dismantling. The spindle should be inserted from the near-side. After tightening the spindle nut, lock the pinch bolt in the near-side fork end.

Removing Rear Wheel (Rigid Frame, 1946 Onwards). Place the machine on the rear stand, and roll back the rubber tube on the

APPENDIX

lead of the rear lamp, so as to expose the brass connection. Break the wire by parting the connector. Then remove the rear mudguard tail piece by taking out the two bolts which secure it to the main portion of the mudguard, also the two bolts at the bottom of the tail piece holding the stays.

Detach the speedometer driving cable. Remove the wheel spindle, distance piece, and speedometer driving box. Next remove the nuts from the hub studs and draw the wheel clear of the three studs, and the wheel will come right away, leaving the brake drum in position.

The procedure for removing the rear wheel, complete with brake drum, is to remove the mudguard tail piece; disconnect the secondary chain; remove the anchorage bolt securing the brake anchorage arm to the frame; loosen the wheel spindle nuts; and then ease the wheel out of the frame fork ends.

Fitting Rear Wheel (Rigid Frame, 1946 Onwards). Proceed in the reverse order of dismantling. Be careful to see that the wheel spindle is hard up against the secondary chain adjusters. See that the chain spring link has the closed end facing the direction of chain movement. Afterwards verify the adjustment of the rear brake.

Removing Rear Wheel (Spring Frame, 1946 Onwards). After placing the machine on the rear stand, detach the mudguard tail piece and the secondary chain. Also disconnect the tail lamp lead at the brass connection. Take off the adjuster nut from the rear brake rod and disconnect the speedometer drive. Slacken both rear wheel spindle nuts and ease the rear wheel out of the fork ends.

Replacing Rear Wheel (Spring Frame, 1946 Onwards). First verify that the spring frame fork ends are lying reasonably parallel to each other. Then position the rear wheel. Ensure that the adjusting stirrup ears are flat against the sides of the fork end and that the cupped adjuster washer is located on the small shoulder at the open end of the fork end slot. Check that the anchor plate on the brake plate enters the slot on the inside of the near-side fork end.

Replace the secondary chain (with closed end facing direction of travel), and tension it with the chain adjusters until there is $\frac{3}{8}$ in. to $\frac{1}{2}$ in. up-and-down movement midway between the chain sprockets. This adjustment *must* be obtained on spring frame models with the weight of the motor-cycle resting on the rear wheel. Finally adjust the rear brake and re-connect the speedometer drive.

Dismantling Rear Hub (Rigid Frame, 1946 Onwards). First remove the rear wheel. Then remove in this order: the locking ring, felt washer, and distance piece, from the plain side of the hub. Drift out the inner sleeve. This will simultaneously detach the single-row bearing. Knock out with a suitable punch the bearing in the brake side of the hub, together with the peened-in washer, felt washer, and pen steel washer.

Dismantling Rear Hub (Spring Frame, 1946 Onwards). Remove the complete rear wheel assembly. Take off the wheel spindle nuts, the adjusting stirrups, the brake plate, speedometer driving box, and the distance pieces. Next remove from the plain side of the hub the locking ring for the ball race. Detach the distance piece and felt washer. Drive out the spindle, bringing with it the single-row bearing fitted to the plain side of the hub. Then drift out the remaining bearing along with the peened-in washer, and the felt and pen steel washers which are fitted into the brake drum side of the hub. If necessary, separate the hub and brake drum. Assemble the rear hub in the reverse order to that given above. Pack the bearings with grease.

Dismantling Front Hub (1946 Onwards). Remove the front wheel after placing the machine on both stands. Detach the brake plate, and its inner and outer distance pieces. Remove the locking ring, felt washer, and distance piece from the opposite side of the hub. Then, with a suitable punch, drive the bearing in the brake side further into the hub, until the single-row bearing comes away. Take out the distance tube and from the same side of the hub, drift out the remaining bearing. The peened-in washer, felt washer, and pen steel washer will come off with this bearing.

Assembling Rear Hub (Rigid Frame, 1946 Onwards). Pack the bearings thoroughly with grease and fit the single-row bearing to the screwed side of the hub. Then fit the inner sleeve, the long end into the single-row bearing. Next replace the distance piece, felt washer, and locking ring. Tighten the latter. Now press into position the double-row bearing, and replace in this order: the pen steel washer; the felt washer; and the dished washer. Rivet the latter lightly into place.

Assembling Front Hub (1946 Onwards). Lubricate the bearings by thoroughly packing them with grease. Press into position the single-row bearing, and then fit the distance piece (with collar abutting the bearing), felt washer, and locking ring. Tighten the latter. Insert through the brake side of the hub the distance tube. See that it beds home against the bearing just fitted. Now

APPENDIX 133

press the double-row bearing into place, and fit the pen steel washer and the felt washer. Afterwards rivet lightly the remaining washer into the recess provided.

Dismantling Brakes (1946 Onwards). First remove the brake plate from the brake drum. Detach the brake lever return spring from the lever. Then remove the nut and washer from the cam spindle. Also remove the brake lever. Remove the cam and its spindle from the bush in the brake plate. Tap the spindle end lightly until the cam clears the shoes. Take off the shoe return springs and remove the circlips which secure the shoes to the

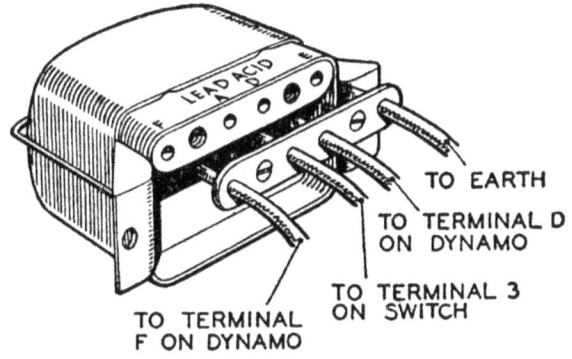

FIG. 69. CUT-OUT AND REGULATOR UNIT CONNECTIONS

pivot pins. Now remove the brake shoes. After removing the nut holding the cam spindle bush to the brake plate, remove the bush.

Assembling Brakes (1946 Onwards). Proceed in the following manner. Fit the cam spindle bush to the brake plate. Then fit the brake shoes and smear a little oil on the pivot pins. Fit *one* shoe to the pivot pin. Then fit the spring (near the pin) to the shoe just fitted. Hold the second shoe close to that already fitted and attach the spring, stretch it, and fit the second shoe to the pivot pin. Now fit the second spring to both brake shoes. Fit the cam spindle to the plate. Separate the shoes with a suitable tool, such as a screwdriver, and allow the cam to pass the ends of the shoes. Fit new circlips to both pivot pins, and assembly is complete. To facilitate the fitting of the circlips, it is advisable to employ a piece of rod (same diameter as the pivot pin) and a piece of tube to fit over the rod.

Removing and Replacing Dynamo. On 1937 and later "Magdyno" models with compensated voltage control, first disconnect the connections from the dynamo terminals. Unscrew the hexagon nut from the "Magdyno" driving end cover. Then loosen the two screws which fasten the band clip. The dynamo can then be withdrawn from the rest of the "Magdyno" unit.

On assembling the dynamo, slide it through the band clip so that the fixing screw passes through the hole in the end cover. See that the gears mesh properly. Tighten the end cover nut and the two band-clip securing screws. Then connect up the connections to the dynamo terminals. Verify that this is correctly done. Referring to Fig. 69, it will be noted that the cable from the cut-out and regulator terminal D is connected to a similarly marked terminal on the dynamo. The same applies to the cut-out and regulator terminal marked F.

Battery Earth Connection. Verify, if any lighting fault occurs, and also periodically, that the battery earth connection is securely fastened.

The Electric Horn. This should not be tampered with unnecessarily, and adjustment is best effected at a Lucas Service Depot. Trouble can be due to a loose connection, a discharged battery, or a short circuit in the horn wiring. Performance may also be spoiled by a loose fixing bolt or by the vibration of an adjacent part. A wiring diagram for 1937 and subsequent Nortons is shown in Fig. 70.

Norton Spares. When ordering spare parts always remember to quote the type of machine, its year of manufacture, and Engine No. or Frame No. (see page 29). Spares can be obtained direct from the Service Dept. of Norton Motors, Ltd., of Bracebridge Street, Birmingham, 6, or from any reputable dealers. Among firms in the London area which keep large stocks of Norton spares may be metnioned Eleanor Motors of 265-269 Mare Street, Hackney, E.8, and Taylor Matterson, Ltd., of 81-83 Bedford Hill, Balham, S.W.12. The former have a specialized Norton Repair Service, and Taylor Matterson, Ltd., always have big stocks of spares available and also special tools of their own design for Norton machines.

Other firms having many branches and handling spares, tools, accessories, clothing, etc., include: The Halford Cycle Co., Ltd., Marble Arch Motor Supplies, Turner's Stores, George Grose, Ltd., and James Grose, Ltd.

APPENDIX

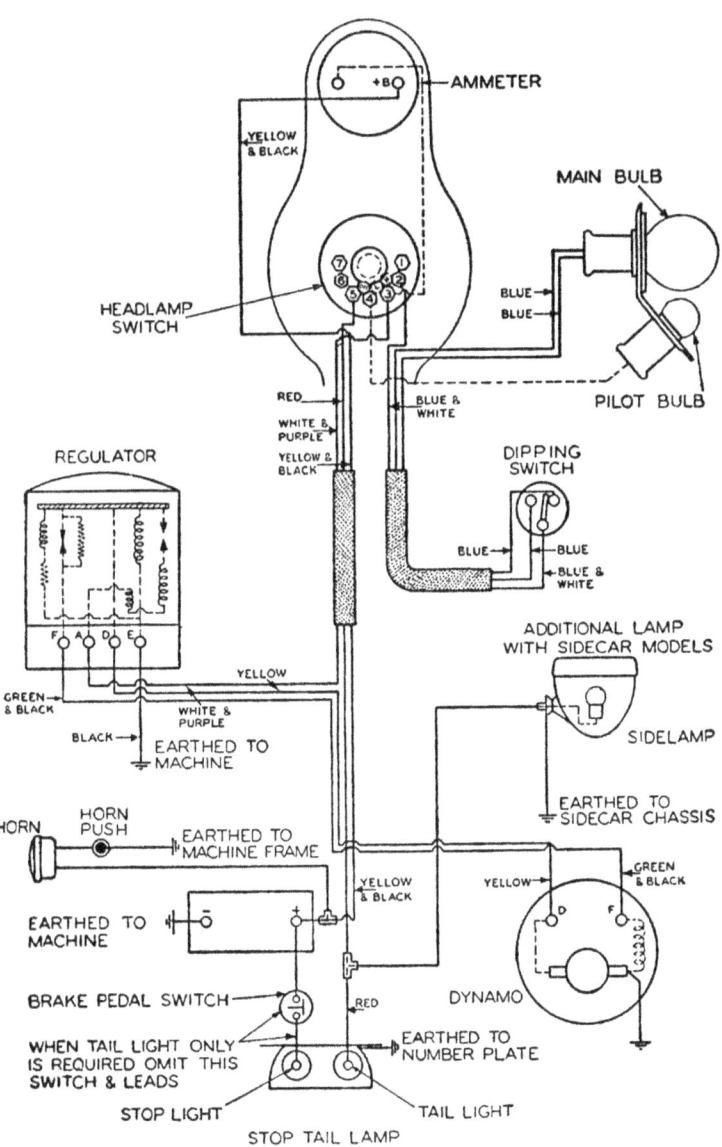

(*Joseph Lucas, Ltd.*)

Fig. 70. Wiring Diagram for 1937-47 Nortons with Lucas "Magdyno," DU Headlamp, and Compensated Voltage Control (no instrument panel)

Wiring diagrams for earlier models are given on pages 56, 58.

INDEX

ACID solution, battery, 53
Advance, ignition, 89
Alinement, wheel, 72
Amal carburettor, 30, 100
—— ——, maintenance, 36
—— ——, tuning, 33, 37, 100
Ammeter, 53, 59

BARREL, cylinder, removing, 74, 111
Battery, care of, 53
—— charging period, 54
Bowden controls, 49, 124
Brakes, 67, 133
Brushes, dynamo, 51
Bulbs, 57

CARBON deposits, 72, 111
——, removing, 79, 111
Chain adjustment, 69
—— case, oil bath, 47, 127
——, magneto, 49
Charging period, battery, 54
Clearance, valve, 61
Clutch adjustment, 65, 117
——, dismantling, 97, 128
Commutator, 50, 52
Compensated voltage control, 59
Contact-breaker, 64, 65, 85
Controls, 20
Crankcase, 46, 116
Cut-out, electro-magnetic, 52, 133
Cycle parts, lubrication of, 46
Cylinder head, removing, 74-77, 111

DAMPER, adjustment, fork, 70
Decarbonizing, 72, 102, 111
Draining crankcase, 46
Dynamo, 46, 50, 133

ENGINE, decarbonizing, 72 111-115
—— lubrication, 17, 44, 101
—— timing, 90-92, 104

FILTER, tank, 45, 102

Focusing headlamps, 55
Fork spindles, 70, 118
Front brake adjustment, 67
—— hub adjustment, 71, 132

GEARBOX, dismantling, 98, 120
Gear changing, 24
—— control adjustment, 66, 130
Grinding-in cylinder head, 82
—— valves, 81, 113

HANDLEBARS, adjusting, 69
High spots, 83
Hub, assembling, 71, 132
—— lubrication, 49

KNOCKING, 24

LUBRICATION chart, 48
"MAGDYNO," Lucas, 50, 89, 104 106
—— lubrication, 46

PEDAL adjustment, brake, 67
Petrol tank, removing, 74, 110
Pilot air adjusting screw, 33, 100
Piston, 74, 78, 114
Primary chain, 47, 69
Push-rods, removing, 76, 112

REAR brakes, adjusting, 67
Rocker arm, contact-breaker, 85
—— box, dismantling, 94, 112
—— —— lubrication, 46
—— —— removing, 76, 112
Rotary gear oil-pump, 41, 106

SECONDARY chain, 47, 69
Shock-absorber, clutch, 97
—— ——, fork, 70
Sidecar alinement, 72
Sparking plug, 25, 63
Spring frame, 118
Steering head, 49, 70, 124

TAPPET adjustment, 61, 102
Telescopic forks, 102, 124
Tyres and wheels, 21, 120, 130

WIRING diagrams, 56, 58, 135

AUTOBOOKS WORKSHOP MANUALS

ALFA ROMEO GIULIA 1300, 1600, 1750, 2000 1962-1978 WSM
BMW 1600 1966-1973 WSM
BMW 2000 & 2002 1966-1976 WSM
BMW 2500, 2800, 3.0 & 3.3 1968-1977 WSM
BMW 316, 320, 320i 1975-1977 WSM
BMW 518, 520, 520i 1973-1981 WSM
FIAT 1100, 1100D, 1100R & 1200 1957-1969 WSM
FIAT 124 1966-1974 WSM
FIAT 124 SPORT 1966-1975 WSM
FIAT 125 & 125 SPECIAL 1967-1973 WSM
FIAT 126, 126L, 126 DV, 126/650 & 126/650 DV 1972-1982 WSM
FIAT 127 SALOON, SPECIAL & SPORT, 900, 1050 1971-1981 WSM
FIAT 128 1969-1982 WSM
FIAT 1300, 1500 1961-1967 WSM
FIAT 131 MIRAFIORI 1975-1982 WSM
FIAT 132 1972-1982 WSM
FIAT 500 1957-1973 WSM
FIAT 600, 600D & MULTIPLA 1955-1969 WSM
FIAT 850 1964-1972 WSM
JAGUAR E-TYPE 1961-1972 WSM
JAGUAR MK 1, 2 1955-1969 WSM
JAGUAR S TYPE, 420 1963-1968 WSM
JAGUAR XK 120, 140, 150 MK 7, 8, 9 1948-1961 WSM
LAND ROVER 1, 2 1948-1961 WSM
MERCEDES-BENZ 190 1959-1968 WSM
MERCEDES-BENZ 220/8 1968-1972 WSM
MERCEDES-BENZ 220B 1959-1965 WSM
MERCEDES-BENZ 230 1963-1968 WSM
MERCEDES-BENZ 250 1968-1972 WSM
MERCEDES-BENZ 280 1968-1972 WSM
MG MIDGET TA-TF 1936-1955 WSM
MINI 1959-1980 WSM
MORRIS MINOR 1952-1971 WSM
PEUGEOT 404 1960-1975 WSM
PORSCHE 911 1964-1973 WSM
PORSCHE 911 1970-1977 WSM
RENAULT 16 1965-1979 WSM
RENAULT 8, 10, 1100 1962-1971 WSM
ROVER 3500, 3500S 1968-1976 WSM
SUNBEAM RAPIER, ALPINE 1955-1965 WSM
TRIUMPH SPITFIRE, GT6, VITESSE 1962-1968 WSM
TRIUMPH TR2, TR3, TR3A 1952-1962 WSM
TRIUMPH TR4, TR4A 1961-1967 WSM
VOLKSWAGEN BEETLE 1968-1977 WSM

VELOCEPRESS AUTOMOBILE BOOKS & MANUALS

ABARTH BUYERS GUIDE
AUSTIN-HEALEY 6-CYLINDER WSM
AUSTIN-HEALEY SPRITE & MG MIDGET 1958-1971 WSM
BMW 600 LIMOUSINE FACTORY WSM
BMW 600 LIMOUSINE OWNERS HAND BOOK & SERVICE MANUAL
BMW ISETTA FACTORY WSM
BOOK OF THE CARRERA PANAMERICANA - MEXICAN ROAD RACE
COMPLETE CATALOG OF JAPANESE MOTOR VEHICLES
DIALED IN - THE JAN OPPERMAN STORY
FERRARI 250/GT SERVICE AND MAINTENANCE
FERRARI 308 SERIES BUYER'S AND OWNER'S GUIDE
FERRARI BERLINETTA LUSSO
FERRARI BROCHURES AND SALES LITERATURE 1946-1967
FERRARI BROCHURES AND SALES LITERATURE 1968-1989
FERRARI GUIDE TO PERFORMANCE
FERRARI OPP, MAINTENANCE & SERVICE H/BOOKS 1948-1963
FERRARI OWNER'S HANDBOOK
FERRARI SERIAL NUMBERS PART I - ODD NUMBERS TO 21399
FERRARI SERIAL NUMBERS PART II - EVEN NUMBERS TO 1050
FERRARI SPYDER CALIFORNIA
FERRARI TUNING TIPS & MAINTENANCE TECHNIQUES
HENRY'S FABULOUS MODEL "A" FORD
HOW TO BUILD A FIBERGLASS CAR
HOW TO BUILD A RACING CAR
HOW TO RESTORE THE MODEL 'A' FORD
IF HEMINGWAY HAD WRITTEN A RACING NOVEL
JAGUAR E-TYPE 3.8 & 4.2 WSM
LE MANS 24 (THE BOOK THAT THE FILM WAS BASED ON)
MASERATI BROCHURES AND SALES LITERATURE
MASERATI OWNER'S HANDBOOK
METROPOLITAN FACTORY WSM
MGA & MGB OWNERS HANDBOOK & WSM
OBERT'S FIAT GUIDE
PERFORMANCE TUNING THE SUNBEAM TIGER
PORSCHE 356 1948-1965 WSM
PORSCHE 912 WSM
SOUPING THE VOLKSWAGEN
TRIUMPH TR2, TR3, TR4 1953-1965 WSM
VEDA ORR'S NEW REVISED HOT ROD PICTORIAL
VOLKSWAGEN TRANSPORTER, TRUCKS, STATION WAGONS WSM
VOLVO 1944-1968 ALL MODELS WSM

BROOKLANDS BOOKS & ROAD TEST PORTFOLIOS (RTP)

AC CARS 1904-2009
ALFA ROMEO 1920-1933 ROAD TEST PORTFOLIO
ALFA ROMEO 1934-1940 ROAD TEST PORTFOLIO
BRABHAM RALT HONDA THE RON TAURANAC STORY
BUGATTI TYPE 10 TO TYPE 40 ROAD TEST PORTFOLIO
BUGATTI TYPE 10 TO TYPE 251 ROAD TEST PORTFOLIO
BUGATTI TYPE 41 TO TYPE 55 ROAD TEST PORTFOLIO
BUGATTI TYPE 57 TO TYPE 251 ROAD TEST PORTFOLIO
DELAHAYE ROAD TEST PORTFOLIO
FERRARI ROAD CARS 1946-1956 ROAD TEST PORTFOLIO
FIAT 500 1936-1972 ROAD TEST PORTFOLIO
FIAT DINO ROAD TEST PORTFOLIO
HISPANO SUIZA ROAD TEST PORTFOLIO
HONDA ST1100/ST1300 PAN EUROPEAN 1990-2002 RTP
JAGUAR MK1 & MK2 ROAD TEST PORTFOLIO
LOTUS CORTINA ROAD TEST PORTFOLIO
MV AGUSTA F4 750 & 1000 1997-2007 ROAD TEST PORTFOLIO
TATRA CARS ROAD TEST PORTFOLIO

VELOCEPRESS MOTORCYCLE BOOKS & MANUALS

AJS SINGLES & TWINS 250cc THRU 1000cc 1932-1948 (BOOK OF)
AJS SINGLES 1955-65 350cc & 500cc (BOOK OF)
AJS SINGLES 1945-60 350cc & 500cc MODELS 16 & 18 (BOOK OF)
ARIEL 1939-1960 4 STROKE SINGLES (BOOK OF)
ARIEL LEADER & ARROW 1958-1964 (BOOK OF)
ARIEL MOTORCYCLES 1933-1951 WSM
ARIEL PREWAR MODELS 1932-1939 (BOOK OF)
BMW M/CYCLES R26 R27 (1956-1967) FACTORY WSM
BMW M/CYCLES R50 R50S R60 R69S (1955-1969) FACTORY WSM
BSA BANTAM (BOOK OF)
BSA ALL FOUR-STROKE SINGLES & V-TWINS 1936-1952 (BOOK OF)
BSA OHV & SV SINGLES - 250cc 1954-1970 (BOOK OF)
BSA OHV & SV SINGLES 1945-54 250-600cc (BOOK OF)
BSA OHV SINGLES 350 & 500cc 1955-1967 (BOOK OF)
BSA PRE-WAR MODELS TO 1939 (BOOK OF)
BSA TWINS 1948-1962 (BOOK OF)
BSA TWINS 1962-1969 (SECOND BOOK OF)
CATALOG OF BRITISH MOTORCYCLES (1951 MODELS)
DOUGLAS PRE-WAR ALL MODELS 1929-1939 (BOOK OF)
DOUGLAS POST-WAR ALL MODELS 1948-1957 FACTORY WSM
DUCATI 160cc, 250cc & 350cc OHC MODELS FACTORY WSM
HONDA 50 ALL MODELS UP TO 1970 INC MONKEY & TRAIL (BOOK OF)
HONDA 90 ALL MODELS UP TO 1966 (BOOK OF)
HONDA MOTORCYCLES 125-150 TWINS C/CS/CB/CA WSM
HONDA MOTORCYCLES 250-305 TWINS C/CS/CB WSM
HONDA MOTORCYCLES C100 SUPER CUB WSM
HONDA MOTORCYCLES C110 SPORT CUB 1962-1969 WSM
HONDA TWINS & SINGLES 50cc THRU 305cc 1960-1966 (BOOK OF)
HONDA TWINS ALL MODELS 125cc THRU 450cc UP TO 1968 (BOOK OF)
INDIAN PONYBIKE, BOY RACER & PAPOOSE ALL PARTS LIST & SALES LIT
LAMBRETTA ALL 125 & 150cc MODELS 1947-1957 (BOOK OF)
LAMBRETTA LI & TV MODELS 1957-1970 (SECOND BOOK OF)
MATCHLESS 350 & 500cc SINGLES 1945-1956 (BOOK OF)
MATCHLESS 350 & 500cc SINGLES 1955-1966 (BOOK OF)
NORTON 1932-1947 (BOOK OF)
NORTON 1938-1956 (BOOK OF)
NORTON DOMINATOR TWINS 1955-1965 (BOOK OF)
NORTON MODELS 19, 50 & ES2 1955-1963 (BOOK OF)
NORTON MOTORCYCLES 1957-1970 FACTORY WSM
NORTON PREWAR MODELS 1932-1939 (BOOK OF)
NSU QUICKLY ALL MODELS 1953-1963 (BOOK OF)
ROYAL ENFIELD SINGLES & V TWINS 1937-1953 (BOOK OF)
ROYAL ENFIELD 736cc INTERCEPTOR FACTORY WSM
ROYAL ENFIELD 250cc & 350cc SINGLES 1958-1966 (SECOND BOOK OF)
SUZUKI 50cc & 80cc UP TO 1966 (BOOK OF)
SUZUKI T10 1963-1967 FACTORY WSM
SUZUKI T20 & T200 1965-1969 FACTORY WSM
TRIUMPH PRE-WAR MOTORCYCLE 1935-1939 (BOOK OF)
TRIUMPH MOTORCYCLES 1937-1951 WSM
TRIUMPH MOTORCYCLES 1945-1955 FACTORY WSM
TRIUMPH TWINS 1956-1969 (BOOK OF)
VELOCETTE ALL SINGLES & TWINS 1925-1970 (BOOK OF)
VESPA 1951-1961 (BOOK OF)
VESPA 125 & 150cc & GS MODELS 1955-1963 (SECOND BOOK OF)
VESPA 90, 125 & 150cc 1963-1972 (THIRD BOOK OF)
VESPA GS & SS 1955-1968 (BOOK OF)
VINCENT MOTORCYCLES 1935-1955 WSM

PLEASE VISIT OUR WEBSITE
www.VelocePress.com
FOR A DETAILED DESCRIPTION
OF ANY OF THESE TITLES

Please check our website:

www.VelocePress.com

for a complete up-to-date list of available titles

www.ingramcontent.com/pod-product-compliance
Lightning Source LLC
Chambersburg PA
CBHW070552170426
43201CB00012B/1818